Spare the Rod

The History and Philosophy of Education Series
Edited by Randall Curren and Jonathan Zimmerman

Spare the Rod

Punishment and the Moral Community of Schools

CAMPBELL F. SCRIBNER AND
BRYAN R. WARNICK

The University of Chicago Press
Chicago and London

The University of Chicago Press, Chicago 60637
The University of Chicago Press, Ltd., London
© 2021 by The University of Chicago
All rights reserved. No part of this book may be used or reproduced in any manner
whatsoever without written permission, except in the case of brief quotations in
critical articles and reviews. For more information, contact the University of Chicago Press,
1427 E. 60th St., Chicago, IL 60637.
Published 2021
Printed in the United States of America

30 29 28 27 26 25 24 23 22 21   1 2 3 4 5

ISBN-13: 978-0-226-78567-7 (cloth)
ISBN-13: 978-0-226-78570-7 (paper)
ISBN-13: 978-0-226-78584-4 (e-book)
DOI: https://doi.org/10.7208/chicago/9780226785844.001.0001

Library of Congress Cataloging-in-Publication Data

Names: Scribner, Campbell F., 1981– author. | Warnick, Bryan R., 1974– author.
Title: Spare the rod : punishment and the moral community of schools /
    Campbell F. Scribner and Bryan R. Warnick.
Other titles: History and philosophy of education.
Description: Chicago ; London : The University of Chicago Press, 2021. |
    Series: The History and philosophy of education series |
    Includes bibliographical references and index.
Identifiers: LCCN 2020046408 | ISBN 9780226785677 (cloth) | ISBN 9780226785707
    (paperback) | ISBN 9780226785844 (ebook)
Subjects: LCSH: School discipline—United States. | School discipline—
    United States—History. | School discipline—Philosophy.
Classification: LCC LB3025 .S37 2021 | DDC 371.50973—dc23
LC record available at https://lccn.loc.gov/2020046408

♾ This paper meets the requirements of ANSI/NISO Z39.48-1992 (Permanence of Paper).

For Alvah: I love you, and hope that you stay out of trouble.—CFS
For Nora, Andrew, Stephen: I see your humanity and see a better world.—BRW

Contents

Perspectives on School Punishment

School discipline and punishment continue to be lightning rods of controversy. We regularly see reports of punishments that seem over the top at best and cruel and unjust at worst. In Georgia, a middle school girl was expelled and had a warrant issued for her arrest because she wrote "Hi" on a school locker.[1] In New Jersey, a kindergartner was suspended for holding his fingers in the shape of a gun.[2] In Oregon, an elementary school forced students who were tardy more than four times to eat their lunch behind a cardboard screen.[3] In Florida, teachers used laws for the treatment of people with mental illnesses to subject uncooperative seven-year-olds to arrest and involuntary psychiatric exams.[4] Black girls have frequently been punished for wearing natural hairstyles or dreadlocks.[5] Children with disabilities, some of them as young as five, have been locked in isolation rooms for hours on end, screaming, for behavior as trivial as throwing Legos or ripping up worksheets.[6] Police officers have regularly handcuffed children for displaying symptoms of autism and have violently subdued middle schoolers "to prove a point" about disrespect.[7] Besides these clear abuses of power, there are other practices that are widely accepted by many schools and communities. Educators commonly employ group or collective punishment, where entire classes are punished for the actions of a few individual students.[8] Corporal punishment, usually involving paddling or spanking students, is still legal in the public schools of nineteen US states (and legal, though rare, in private schools in forty-eight states). In those states that allow corporal punishment, 14 percent of public schools actually engage in the practice.[9] Less sensational, but much more common, are exclusionary punishments, such as suspension and expulsion, which remove allegedly misbehaving students from classrooms and schools, either temporarily or permanently. Perhaps most troubling, as we shall see, are reports of the gender and racial disparities in the administration of school punishment.[10] The US Government Accountability Office (GAO) has found that boys, Black students, and special education students are punished far more frequently than other students. These disparities hold true across many different types of schools and socioeconomic contexts.[11] Combined with an increased police presence in schools, these disparities seem to involve schools in what has been called a "school-to-prison pipeline," in which students of color are channeled away from educational institutions and toward the criminal justice system.

Despite a growing body of research about the detrimental effects of these practices, some commentators continue to claim that schools are "going soft" on discipline and that violence and chaos are the result. They believe that schools have become more "progressive" and "student centered," emphasizing students' feelings over learning, therapy over discipline, and the accommodation of wrongdoers over the protection of victims. For these critics, anecdotal accounts of school violence attest to the failure of contemporary approaches, and a return to strict discipline and exacting punishments is essential for keeping schools ordered and safe.[12]

Commentators on the other side of the issue voice serious moral and educational criticisms of punishment, not only regarding its severity but also regarding its principle. Some reject the whole idea of punishment, viewing it simply as an act of revenge and violence and arguing that to intentionally harm a child is a relic of a barbaric past that human beings should abandon and denounce. In the case of children, to whatever degree immoral or criminal behavior is a matter of brain chemistry or involuntary trauma rather than free choice, the notion of punishment as "getting what you deserve" seems like an inappropriate response. There are others, as we will see, who argue that punishment is inherently anti-educational. Education is about building students' capacity to understand the moral reasoning behind their behavior. Yet many forms of punishment do not engage reason but impose sanctions through blunt force. Critics point to psychological research suggesting that this sort of punishment does not fundamentally change student behavior and that any apparent change in behavior evaporates after the threat of punishment is removed. There is nothing educational about that.

What should we make of these debates? The goal of this book is to give readers a sense of *perspective* on school punishment by exploring the various meanings of punishment in schools, how these meanings have changed over time, and how a deeper understanding of these meanings can shape schools in the future. Part of our discussion will investigate punishment as a general human phenomenon and ask how it might be applied (or misapplied) to the particular setting of schools and to children, who are still developing judgment and character. Another part of our discussion will look at schools in the past, exploring how teachers administered punishment and how their actions were a response to larger cultural forces. Finally, we will consider contemporary data about schools and punishment, how punishment affects children, and what unintended consequences punishment might have.

We believe that philosophical and historical perspectives on punishment will be useful to those who must make educational decisions—namely, teachers and administrators, as well as policy makers who shape the structure of school environments. Educators face the difficult job of teaching challenging and unfamiliar material, maintaining classroom order and safety, and fostering caring and humane relationships with students who are going through the difficult process of growing up, often under conditions of poverty and racism. We recognize the complexity of these educational tasks. While teachers can certainly refine their practices from an ethical perspective (and we hope this book helps in that regard), they also need the support of a wider public, a public that understands the underlying issues and gives teachers the resources and moral support they need to practice their craft in a just and caring way. Too often, courts, legislators, school boards, and local voters have tolerated unjust forms of punishment on the basis of questionable legal theories, misguided notions of tradition, or a vague deference to "local control" or professional expertise. We hope that this book advances a wider conversation about school punishment in the public sphere—that students, scholars, citizens, and policy makers will look frankly at what schools have been, what they currently are, and what they should be, with the goal of thinking more clearly together about the purposes of school punishment.

To say that the goal of this book is to gain "perspective" on punishment is to say very little in itself. To clarify, we note a number of smaller goals that will contribute to that perspective. The first goal is to understand how punishment might be defined, how it might differ from "discipline," what ethical issues it presents, and what sorts of tools exist for thinking through issues of punishment in school. In particular, we want to explore the idea that punishment is communicative—that it sends certain messages about moral responsibility, human action, problem-solving, and community norms. Critics have important points to make about the questionable educational value of school punishment, but we believe there is a role for punishment when it allows certain conversations to take place that would not be possible otherwise. Seeking perspective on punishment requires that we develop a clear understanding of an often ambiguous term, paying close attention to areas where punishment is legitimately contested and problematic.

Accordingly, chapter 1 will address some of the ethical and conceptual is-sues involved with punishment, drawing from important philosophical work on "punishment" as a general concept in human societies. The chapter con-tains a number of important reflective tools for those interested in an ethics of school punishment. Of particular importance will be what has been called the "expressive function" of punishment—that is, that punishment is a means for the community to communicate moral disapproval of an action and an actor. Punishment occurs, in a technical sense, when a message of moral con-cern (a condemnation) is present. This sort of communication transcends what can be communicated verbally. Indeed, sometimes merely talking about serious misbehavior with a student is not "symbolically adequate" to capture the gravity of what has occurred. By giving a symbolically adequate expres-sion of disapproval, a punishment allows for certain sorts of conversations to take place, certain sorts of remorse to be shown, and certain sorts of apologies to be given. The communicative nature of punishment gives the practice a fundamentally educational element, one that goes beyond simple displays of power by teachers, and speaks to some of the objections made by the critics of punishment. This does not mean, however, that all school management techniques constitute punishment: many strategies rightly reward students or impose various sorts of sanctions without implicating moral questions. Nor does a vindication of school punishment mean that all types of punishment are justified in all contexts. Particular punishment practices, we argue, have "secondary expressions" that go beyond the message of general disapproval. At the end of chapter 1, we point to three areas where these secondary ex-pressions have particularly troubling implications: the use of corporal pun-ishment, the disparities that exist in the use of punishment among different student populations, and exclusionary forms of punishment.

Having established a working definition of punishment and introduced aspects that we find problematic, the book then helps readers understand how we arrived at our current situation—that is, the book demonstrates how con-ceptions, applications, and justifications of punishment have changed over time. Chapter 2 traces schooling in the United States from the seventeenth to the nineteenth centuries, a period during which small one-room schools serving mostly agrarian communities evolved into hierarchically organized systems spanning entire cities, tasked with instilling strong morals and a ro-bust national identity in their students. Accompanying these changes were three primary forms of punishment, which we, in turn, associate with three different visions of American society. Corporal punishment, the earliest and most widespread method, derived from patriarchal worldviews and was pop-ular among traditionalists, religious conservatives, and rural communities.

Public shaming, which we associate with various forms of liberalism, replaced physical pain with peer pressure and competition and was popular in market-oriented cities. Gentler forms of moral suasion emerged with a feminized and increasingly professional teaching force and paralleled Romantic ideals of the middle-class family. While all three of these approaches continue (somewhat haphazardly) in American schools today, examination of their use in the seventeenth, eighteenth, and nineteenth centuries offers the opportunity to see them as distinct systems of social organization, each with its own assumptions about human nature, adult authority, and the basis of self-government.

While we object to the secondary expressions that accompanied some forms of punishment in the past, we appreciate that punishment's primary expression was generally robust—that is, that schools communicated moral disapproval in ways that demanded public debate and deliberation. Schools were, in their way, a part of a moral conversation. Chapter 3 argues that while the professionalization of teaching and administration during the twentieth century moderated punishment in some ways, it also subordinated this type of public accountability to the judgment of self-proclaimed experts. Professional educators pioneered a new language of emotional sensitivity and self-regulation and replaced painful or degrading punishments with more neutral forms of physical separation, including suspensions. In the process, however, they reduced punishment to a management technique, stripped of its moral overtones. The new approaches did nothing to challenge traditional notions of classroom order, nor did they mitigate the entrenched prejudices of students, teachers, and administrators. These issues became clear as child labor laws pushed more working-class students into school and as immigration and desegregation brought more students of color into contact with racist teachers (and, as early as the 1950s, with uniformed police officers). By the 1960s, obviously discriminatory instances of suspension and corporal punishment began to provoke legal challenges, which attempted to counterbalance teachers' professional prerogative with safeguards for students' rights. Yet almost all of these challenges failed. Courts deferred to local administrators on appropriate standards of punishment, overlooking the ways in which schools were increasingly immune from democratic authority. While courts alone cannot end inequalities in school punishment, we argue that they can spur meaningful debate by scrutinizing the effects of local policies rather than applying inflexible tests and outdated notions of school governance in their decisions. With the rise of suspensions and "zero tolerance" policies, we worry that bureaucratic procedures, under the guise of professionalism, have actually encouraged inflexibility, lack of judgment, and a breakdown between schools and the communities they serve.

Readers should note two important caveats to this historical narrative. First, it is important to remember that any discussion of "school punishment" imposes arbitrary limits on the causes of and responses to youthful misbehavior, much of which takes place outside of school walls. Adults exercise authority over children in many arenas, most of which lack what we call the "special characteristics" of schools, which are segregated by age (unlike workplaces), perform explicitly educative functions (unlike courts or the police), and are required to serve public interests (unlike families or religious congregations). The latter institutions appear at the edges of our narrative, sometimes cooperating and at other times competing with schools for the right to punish children, but it is beyond the scope of our argument to describe each of them in detail. By the same logic, descriptions of "school punishment" necessarily exclude children who are not in schools. During the eighteenth and nineteenth centuries, the United States established perhaps the most extensive educational system in the world. Proponents extolled it as an engine of democratic citizenship, but it also reflected much of the era's White supremacy. Children of the enslaved and the dispossessed came in for their share of state-sanctioned violence, but, as state and local governments cut off educational opportunities for Native American, Mexican American, and African American residents, much of that violence initially took place outside of schools. Children with disabilities faced similar challenges, subject to physical restraint and isolation at home or in special institutions rather than in mainstream classrooms. Thus, while the forms of punishment that chapter 2 discusses were not racially determined—segregated schools confronted many of the same debates about punishment as their White counterparts—the disproportionate punishment of children experiencing poverty, children with disabilities, and children of color in chapter 3 should be seen as an extension of earlier forms of control and surveillance (by the police, among others) that took place outside of schools before following their targets into the school building.

A second point to bear in mind is that "punishment" has never been a uniform phenomenon in American schools. While we offer a general overview of the ways that schools corrected children, practices varied significantly between particular regions and eras and differed according to the identities of teachers and students, the organization of classrooms, prevailing public sentiment, and broader economic and political structures. Worse, educators did not always observe the philosophical categories that we establish, mischaracterizing some forms of misbehavior as moral transgressions when they were not, leaching other forms of their appropriate moral significance, and inflicting punishments far out of proportion to children's wrongdoings—issues that are still present in many contemporary schools. We emphasize this complexity at the outset, not to confuse readers but to challenge any easy assumptions about the superiority of schools in either the past or the present. Ours is not a story of progress, chronicling ever gentler or more humane treatment of students, as some readers might expect. Nor is it a story of decline, in which the prohibition of stricter punishments unleashed chaos, disrespect, and violence in the schools, as others might worry. It is, rather, a story of contingency and competing visions of American society. In short, it is a call for discernment.

Chapter 4 builds on the historical analysis of the preceding two chapters and on the expressive role of punishment described in chapter 1 to defend a vision of what punishment in schools should look like. Indeed, the last goal of the book is to present an argument for an approach to punishment that best matches the aims and purposes of schooling. Doing so requires clarity about the educational goals that schools should pursue, about the responsibilities of schools in liberal-democratic societies, about the pressures that are placed on such schools, and about the resources schools need to accomplish their goals. Taking all of this into account, we ask, How should schools punish students? We have seen that early American schools' emphasis on moral formation and ordered classrooms, enforced through corporal punishment, was largely replaced by systems of bureaucratic control emphasizing therapy, behavioral management, and exclusionary punishments. Neither of these historical approaches captures the sort of moral community that schools should be. We describe a more compelling vision of the school community by analyzing the "special characteristics" of schools—those aspects of schools that make them unique and define their role. We then argue for a way of thinking about punishment that matches the moral community of schools, correctly described. This approach to punishment is what has been called the "restorative justice" approach. It takes advantage of the expressive function of punishment to produce a dialogue among students and teachers that is aimed at repairing broken relationships. This dialogue transforms school discipline into an educational process, capturing the idea that schools should be focused on teaching and learning. We end the book, then, by offering an alternative paradigm of discipline and punishment that better aligns with a proper vision of schools as moral communities. This paradigm emphasizes the roles of mutual recognition, dialogue, problem-solving, and community involvement and does justice to the notion of children as growing moral agents.

Discipline and punishment are perhaps the most ethically fraught issues confronting our education system today. Students misbehave for innumerable reasons, sometimes asserting legitimate claims to personal dignity or political resistance; sometimes acting out of impulsivity, misunderstanding, or immaturity; sometimes breaking rules for reasons entirely outside their control; and sometimes willfully violating the rights of others. How schools respond to these transgressions can determine children's relationships with their classmates and teachers, their self-concept, and their ability to pursue their life goals, not to mention the safety and academic success of their classmates. Schools must ensure that students, teachers, parents, policy makers, and the public all perceive punishment as effective and fair. Punishment is a complicated practice and one that schools need to get right. Yet far too often they fail. Especially troubling is that they fail in ways that undermine basic tenets of moral culpability, civic equality, and restitution or reform. This book represents our effort to clarify the purposes of punishment, to identify the sources of its misapplication, and to reaffirm schools as moral communities, thereby charting a better course of correction in the future.

There is, in fact, much to gain from thinking deeply about punishment and discipline in the context of American schooling. Legal scholar David Garland asks us to acquire a more detailed "appreciation of the nature of punishment, of its character as a social institution, and of its role in social life."[13] As we think about punishment, we learn not only about disciplinary practices but also much about our values, our communities, our relationships, and our sense of ourselves as moral agents. As philosopher Rob Canton states, "Punishment instructs us about right and wrong, about agency and responsibility, it teaches about authority."[14] Accordingly, thinking carefully about punishment in schools is important not only because of the need to examine the ethics of punishment practices but also because reflection opens a window onto our assumptions about education in general. Thinking about punishment and discipline in schools forces us to think about the nature of education, the role of the teacher, social authority, moral responsibility, and childhood, among many other things. We hope that readers find this book useful in their own thinking about the nature of schooling in democratic societies.

Punishment: Its Meaning and Justification

When considering punishment and discipline in schools, two preliminary sets of questions demand careful consideration. The first set involves questions of *meaning*. What counts as "punishment" in schools? How are the concepts of "punishment" and "discipline" different, if they are? What purposes are punishment and discipline supposed to be serving in schools? And what can punishment practices in schools tell us about our broader assumptions about education? The second set of questions involves the *justification* of punishment and discipline in schools. Are public school educators ever justified in punishing or disciplining students? Are these things essential to, say, moral education? Or, are punishment and discipline fundamentally opposed to education? If punishment (or some specific form of punishment) is justified in schools, what ethical guidelines should direct the administration of punishment?

In this chapter, we offer a preliminary sketch of the conceptual, moral, and educational terrain of discipline and punishment in schools. The conceptual and justificatory questions broached in this first chapter highlight some areas of interest that will be addressed in subsequent chapters. This chapter also introduces critical issues to consider in constructing an ethics of punishment. The goal is not to raise questions for the sake of abstract understanding but to ask questions that can serve as "reflective tools" that educators and citizens can use in thinking critically about school punishment. These inquiries will help those interested in schools to achieve a greater degree of clarity about the nature of punishment, when and how it might be appropriate, and what reasons might justify it.

The Nature and Meaning of Punishment

What types of actions constitute a "punishment" in schools? Consider the following cases:

1. A student does not study and is given a low score on an exam.
2. Students vandalize a soda machine, and as a "natural consequence" the machine is not replaced.
3. A student is moved to a different seat, away from a group of friends where disruptive talking occurs.
4. A student violates the protocol on a chemistry experiment, setting something on fire, and the student is then required to write an essay on the danger of chemical reactions.
5. A student is suffering from mental illness and lashes out violently against other students and is separated into a special classroom.

Which of these cases count as "punishment," if any? In addressing this question, perhaps it might help to think about what punishment might mean outside of school contexts. Various definitions have been proposed in the scholarly literature. In what has been called the "received view" of punishment, punishment is defined as the authorized and intentional imposition of something unwanted (a pain, hardship, or burden) on an individual (namely, the offender) because that individual has violated a socially sanctioned rule (committed an offense).[1] Nearly every word of this definition is important in understanding what punishment is and what it is not. It involves a hardship, administered to an individual by the social authority, because of undesired conduct by that individual. Thus, a student berating another student on social media is not "punishing" the other student, according to this definition, because she lacks social authority. This might be an act of vengeance for a past disagreement, but it is not punishment. Likewise, implementing hardship on another when no offense has occurred is better thought of as persecution of some sort, not punishment. The imposition of something unwanted must be *for* the offense and not simply occasioned by the punishment.[2] That is, the punishment must be because of the action that was performed.

A few things to notice about the "received view" definition of punishment we are using. First, the intentions and perceptions of the people involved matter a great deal. Identifying cases of punishment requires interpretation. The idea of a "hardship," for example, is somewhat subjective. Opinions differ on what a hardship is and is not; thus, what is considered a punishment to one person might not be considered punishment to another. This difference in perception might be particularly pronounced across cultural differences and age discrepancies. Some actions of a teacher may be perceived as a hardship by students, but for a teacher they count more as a learning exercise (extra homework for poor performance on an exam, for example). The role of intentions also makes a difference in understanding punishment and discipline in school settings insofar as punishment constitutes an intentional imposition of suffering or hardship on another. Nathan Hanna states, "To punish an offender, one must aim to hurt or harm her in some way; the treatment to which she is subjected must be used at least in part as a way of making her suffer."[3] While the explicit intention to hurt others may be justified in some rare cases (e.g., self-defense), critics see this intention to harm as a reason to consider punishment as something intrinsically objectionable, a persistent remnant of past barbarism in human life, and believe that deliberately causing harm to others is something we should always try to avoid.[4] For the critics, this intention is particularly troublesome in the cases of youth and children in schools. An explicit intent to cause children harm is even more objectionable because of children's vulnerability and lack of full moral responsibility. Others would counter, and we would agree, that some forms of hardship are much more objectionable than others—the critics' blanket condemnation of intentional hardship is much too blunt. Requiring someone who has vandalized a school to pay a fine or clean the school intentionally imposes a hardship or burden, but it hardly feels like a relic of barbarism. Still, the critics have a point: it is important to take the nature of children into account, which is something we will develop throughout this book. Abstract philosophical theories of punishment need to take children seriously.

Another thing to notice about the definition of punishment is that the notion of social authority can be fairly complex, particularly in schools. Theories of punishment tend to focus on the state legal apparatus as having the only legitimate authority to punish for the violation of law.[5] In reality, though, what we call "punishment" occurs in many settings, including in families, religious organizations, schools, and so forth. The relationship between punishment and legitimate social authority is an important one, which we will revisit. For now, we can point out that the authority to punish is constructed in different ways in different educational environments. In some cases, schools may, for better or worse, relinquish a degree of social authority to parents, law enforcement, or even students themselves. An interesting case is Summerhill School in Suffolk, England, where student punishment is decided by a student and teacher deliberating body. In other cases, as we will see, educators have relinquished control of disciplinary matters to law enforcement and policy makers, often with troubling results.

The Expressive Function of Punishment:
Moral Communication

When thinking about the meaning of punishment, we should also note what has been called the "expressive function" of punishment. One of the defining features of punishment is that it is expressive—it sends a message of disapproval of an action or actor. It is an act of blaming or, perhaps, of moral education.[6] This function connects punishment quite strongly to the tasks of teaching and learning. Punishment transmits a message of judgment against the offender and condemns what the offender has done. Punishment is, in other words, an act of communication, conveying what words alone cannot. Joel Feinberg notes that there are some forms of social control that do not involve this element of moral blame and judgment. For this reason, he distinguishes a punishment from a penalty.[7] A punishment expresses moral blame against an offender, while a penalty seems to lack this element. Generally speaking, no *moral* statement is made against someone who is missing a license plate on their automobile. A license plate is itself not a moral concern. Rather, the penalty of the traffic ticket is a form of social control meant to efficiently manage what can be a messy and contested social circumstance. In schools, similarly, we might separate students who are talking during class (a penalty), not because socializing is morally wrong but because it impedes the goals of the larger social situation.

In education, a related distinction is often made between "discipline" and "punishment."[8] Similar to a penalty, discipline typically involves correcting a behavior that is inappropriate to a classroom, without concern for judging or changing the moral character of the student. For example, for those who use this distinction, delaying recess for students who leave their chairs during class time would be an act of discipline. The act of leaving one's chair is not a moral failure; rather, it is breaking a rule that allows classroom work to proceed efficiently. In contrast, "punishment" occurs when a moral offense has transpired that goes beyond school rules. A true punishment is intended to express moral disapproval of the action and, perhaps, anger and disgust at the actor.[9] Bullying, sexual harassment, and racial targeting would be moral offenses that might deserve punishment in this sense, because the wrongness of these actions involves more than simply breaking school conventions that preserve social efficiency.

Determining whether the distinction between discipline and punishment is tenable requires further exploration. On one hand, it does seem like the distinction between an action that violates moral norms and an action that violates school conventions is an important and helpful one. The distinction may suggest different reactions and distinct forms of response depending on the level of "morality" that is involved in an action. On the other hand, school norms, school conventions, and efficient school operations are themselves not without moral weight. If violating class rules by leaving one's chair impedes the learning of other students, then this action has in some sense harmed those students or perhaps even violated their rights in some way. The action might be disrespectful to these other students and to the teacher in a morally troubling manner. Indeed, it might be intentionally insolent, explicitly meant to denigrate a teacher or classmate. In this way, a violation of classroom rules certainly enters into a moral calculus and, thus, the distinction between discipline and punishment may break down under close scrutiny, particularly when we consider the moral status of the school community.

For these reasons, Joan Goodman helpfully divides the universe of discipline into three categories: the moral, the derivatively moral, and the conventional.[10] Student behavior that violates school conventions should be handled through management tactics, like sanctions and penalties, or may simply point to the need for joint problem-solving. In contrast, student behavior that violates moral norms requires punishment, which involves this expressive function of disapproval. Goodman, however, recognizes the complexity with the category of the "derivatively moral." This category involves behaviors that are not in themselves immoral (like being tardy) but are performed on the part of students with the intention to show contempt or insolence for others. Sometimes the violation of school rules and conventions can become an indirect vehicle for immoral action. In many cases, perhaps even in most cases, no disrespect is intended by such behavior—violations of school rules like tardiness may occur for valid nonmoral reasons, and these can be figured out as educators adopt more of a problem-solving mode rather than through moral criticism. Determining whether a behavior like tardiness is a violation of school convention or an indirect, derivatively immoral action involves delicate interpretation of the will and intent of the student, which are not always obvious.[11]

A problem in schools, Goodman states, is that these distinctions are ignored. Simple violations of convention are taken as moral failings, worthy of punishment, when no morally problematic intention was behind them. Or, sometimes, even plainly moral offenses, like cheating, are taken as issues of management—that is, as Goodman says, a time for "disciplinary response," "interventions," "options," and "measures"[12] (we argue later that, historically, the trend has been in this direction, moving away from addressing these issues as moral problems). Goodman rightly calls for greater clarity on the part of educators. A thoughtful distinction between discipline and punishment opens up productive lines of inquiry: What is the nature of the behavior—is it a violation of school convention or of moral norms? If it is a violation of convention, how can the underlying cause be addressed? If it is a violation of moral norms, how can the proper message be sent, from the perspective of moral education? If there are suspicions of disrespect and insolence behind conventional rule breaking, are they grounded in solid evidence? And how might the educator's response—in terms of severity, tone, and explanation—be tailored depending on the answers to these questions? An ethic of punishment requires that immoral action be addressed differently than violations of school conventions.

The Role of Hardships and Burdens in Moral Dialogue

For now, we will focus on immoral student behavior and turn to the important question of why messages of disapproval in education would entail the "hard treatment" of punishment. Why not just use words to criticize the behavior of students, explaining to them why their actions were morally wrong? Perhaps the rough treatment involved in punishment is, after all, just a relic of barbarism that we should seek to eliminate in education. For proponents of punishment, the answer is that punishment communicates disapproval in a way that words alone cannot. Christopher Bennett, for example, argues that punishment expresses disapproval in a way that is "symbolically adequate" to the wrongs that have been committed.[13] Suppose it was decided that society wanted to condemn sexual assault on campus and further decided to punish the offenders by writing them a strongly worded letter alerting them to the gravity of what they had done. The letter outlines the harm that has been caused and chastises the offender. For most people, sending such a letter of disapproval would not be a statement of sufficient strength, given the nature of the offense and the gravity of sexual assault. A letter would not be symbolically adequate to speak to the harm that has occurred.

Bill Wringe, for his part, takes a "denunciatory" view of expressive punishment.[14] He argues that the burden or hardship imposed by punishment alerts the community that certain kinds of norms are important and serious. A strongly worded letter does not sufficiently alert the community to the seriousness of sexual assault. Something more is needed. In an educational context, R. S. Peters suggests that the burdens imposed by punishment in schools might bring adolescents "to their senses" by "focusing awareness on social realities."[15] Educators concerned about, say, bullying might want to send a stronger message about bullying or sexual harassment than words of reprimand alone can capture, to underscore the importance of the "social realities" that students may not be privy to. After all, we learn the seriousness of our social actions not simply from what people say in response to what we have done but also from what they do in response. The hard treatment of punishment is an action that, going beyond words, conveys moral gravity. Such treatment constructs a community message. It highlights and emphasizes, underscores and accentuates.

The notion of an expressive function of punishment, we believe, illuminates a possible role of punishment in educational settings. To state the matter a bit more formally, we first recognize that education is fundamentally a communicative process, a dialogue between developing children or youth and the larger community. Part of what should be communicated through education are norms governing the moral life of the community. For some wrongs, however, words of explanation alone cannot demonstrate with sufficient strength the community concern; therefore, some sort of *action* on the part of educators is required to convey the proper message. An action that is fully adequate to speak to the wrongdoing may sometimes involve imposing a burden or something undesirable on students. In such cases, we have a valid use of the expressive function of punishment, with punishment playing a role in the communicative project of the school, initiating students into the moral life of the community. Recognizing this expressive function reveals the proper role for punishment in educational settings.

As we think about how the expressive function of punishment can apply in specific situations, it may be helpful to consider the audience of the message that is being conveyed. The first possible audience of the expressive message is the offender. The expression is aimed at getting an offender to realize that a wrong has been committed and, thereafter, feel remorse. The ultimate goal, in many cases, is the moral reformation of the offender through the expressive message of punishment. One of the leading theorists of the expressive theory of punishment, Antony Duff, argues that punishment is part of a dialogue between the community and the offender, where the community expresses disapproval and the offender is given the opportunity to offer penance. The act of punishment—the burden or harm that is imposed on the offender—is important for Duff because (again) words alone are not enough to express the moral gravity of certain actions. Notably, though, punishment does not simply allow the community to express outrage; it also allows the offender to make a much deeper statement of remorse by embracing the punishment, using it as an act of penance. Duff notes,

> Sometimes, however, a (mere) apology is not enough. If I have done a serious wrong to another person, I cannot expect to settle or resolve the matter merely

by apologizing to him: something more than that is due to him and from me. This is not because a serious wrong is likely to involve some material harm for which compensation must also be paid. Some such wrongs (serious betrayals of a friendship or a marriage, for instance) involve no such harm, while some harms (the harm involved in a rape or in a fraud committed by a friend, for instance) cannot be made good by material compensation. The point is rather that the victim cannot reasonably be expected to forgive me, to treat the matter as closed, merely on receipt of a verbal apology, however sincere, and that the wrongdoer cannot reasonably expect to close the matter thus. The wrong goes too deep for that. It goes too deep for the victim. . . . It also goes too deep for the wrongdoer, whether or not she realizes it. To think that she could just apologize, and then return to her normal life, would be to portray the wrong as a relatively trivial matter that did not seriously damage the victim or their relationship.[16]

Duff recognizes that some harms go "too deep" for simple apologies on the part of offenders. A hardship imposed by punishment (a prison sentence) gives the offender an opportunity for the message of disapproval to "go deep"; at the same time, the sentence gives the offender the opportunity to show remorse in a way that goes beyond a simple apology.[17] Punishment, then, opens up opportunities for reconciliation between the offender and the victim. Punishment plays a role in *making* some statements of hurt, remorse, and apology meaningful. Punishment not only allows the community voice to be symbolically adequate; it also allows the offender's apology to be symbolically adequate. It opens up two-way communication to remorse and reintegration.

The second possible audience for the expressive function of punishment is not so much the offender but the larger community. It could be a classroom, an entire school, or even those on the outside. The point of the expressive punishment is to denounce a particular action, and the harsh treatment gives the denunciation depth and power. Wringe argues that this view on the audience of punishment holds several advantages.[18] For one thing, it distances the social authority from the overt *intention* to harm, which is so problematic from a moral point of view. An offender is given a burden, yes, and the burden is not an accidental feature of the punishment, but the intention in the first instance is not to cause suffering but to highlight an action for the community. Wringe also argues that his "denunciatory view" better deals with two important problems with punishment: why punishment should be public and why harsh treatment is justified. If the point of punishment is to make a statement about the types of norms that society takes seriously, then it clearly does need to be public. If the point of punishment is to send a strong message about moral norms, then this justifies harsh treatment in order to be taken seriously.

In developing an ethical approach to punishment, we must think carefully about the audience of punishment, if a punishment is to be given. If there is a message to be sent from punishment, who exactly is the intended audience? Is it the student offender? The victims? The larger school community? There are certain times when a specific punishment should be confidential—students are still learning and growing, after all, and public knowledge of misbehavior might harm them unnecessarily outside of their schools or in their future lives. There may be other circumstances, however, requiring that punishment be more widely known. Perhaps victims need to know that the school takes their pain seriously and that something is being done about a given problem. This is particularly true of behavior that has been ignored or covered up in the past. If a student is sexually assaulted by another student, the offender's punishment might be an important thing for the victim as well as the larger school community to know about. Or it may be that schools want to make sure their students and the larger community know that, for example, racial slurs are not tolerated within the school. Such publicity may be necessary to change the culture and to show that the school is taking certain behaviors seriously. The publicity that should be given to punishment is heightened when we consider, as we soon will, the question of racial disparities. If punishment sends a message to the community, as it does under the expressive theory of punishment, then unfair or inequitable punishment practices also send a message. These messages call the broader legitimacy of schools and other social institutions into question. Educators should carefully consider the expressive function of punishment and also the expressive nature of *unfair* punishment.

We could also ask more questions about what punishment is intended to express. Part of the expression may be how the community feels about the action and the perpetrator. That is, it may be that punishment is intended to send a message of emotional disapproval. Thom Brooks lists a number of possible emotions that the community might be trying to express with punishment.[19] These emotions include anger, fear, and disgust at what has occurred. Brooks notes the problems with thinking that punishment communicates a community emotion, among them the fact that different people have different emotional reactions to crimes. This is true even within relatively homogeneous communities. In diverse and complex liberal-democratic societies, the problem is compounded. There is no "one voice" by which the community speaks, no one emotion that is communicated. Still, the expressive view does capture something important—namely, that punishment practices often express the emotions of a community (albeit a diverse set of emotions) and that part of what a society wants is for offenders to understand the anger and fear that they have aroused. It may be that punishment in school settings gives students a feel for the emotional response that certain actions will provoke from the larger community; in effect, it allows students to enter the social and emotional consciousnesses of their communities.

Under the topic of the expressive function of punishment, we should note the existence of what we call "secondary expressions" of punishment. The "general" expression of punishment is moral disapproval on the part of the community. A "secondary" expression is a message conveyed by the specific type of punishment practice. Specific types of punishment can send messages above and beyond those of a general moral disapproval. They can amplify the disapproval in certain ways; or, they can send additional messages about relationships, authority, the self, and moral responsibility. Often, these messages are unintended, and many are injurious. For example, as we will see, physical punishment seems to send a message about the appropriateness of using physical force to solve social problems. Suspension and expulsion practices seem to send messages about belonging, about one's place (or lack thereof) in the school community. One challenge of punishment and discipline in education is making sure the secondary expressions of punishment consistently align with the other messages that the school is trying to send. The secondary messages should agree with the school's educational mission and with its vision of what it means for students to develop as individuals and citizens. In the remainder of the book, this alignment will be something we seek to find.

Applying the "Expressive Function" in Education

Recall, again, the definition of punishment: the authorized and intentional imposition of something unwanted (a pain, hardship, or burden) on an individual (namely, the offender) because that individual has violated a socially sanctioned rule (committed an offense). We can take this definition, add the notion that there is an "expressive function" to punishment, and return to the cases that were previously presented. It immediately becomes clear that what happens in schools often exists in a sort of gray area between being a "punishment" and being something else. Here, again, are the cases:

1. A student does not study and is given a low score on an exam.
2. Students vandalize a soda machine, and as a "natural consequence" the machine is not replaced.

3. A student is moved to a different seat, away from a group of friends where disruptive talking occurs.
4. A student violates the protocol on a chemistry experiment, setting something on fire, and the student is then required to write an essay on the danger of chemical reactions.
5. A student is suffering from mental illness and lashes out violently against other students and is separated into a special classroom.

These cases highlight a number of issues surrounding punishment in schools. Is the lower grade given in case 1 a form of punishment? Many would probably say that this does not count as a punishment: the student is merely given what that student has earned. We see now that whether this is a punishment would partly depend on what message is being sent by grades and to whom, and also whether the expressed message involves moral disapproval. Is the lower grade intended as an explicit communication to students that they need to work harder? Or is it simply a report on a level of academic achievement, free from moral messages—a sort of penalty? Clearly, grades function in numerous ways, and sometimes (rightly or wrongly) they act as moral communications to students about their effort. To the extent that grades explicitly include things like effort and "participation," they have a moral dimension. The lowering of a grade could be at least sometimes considered "hard treatment," conveying a moral message, and therefore, sometimes, an avenue for punishment.

Consider also the idea of letting students experience the "natural consequences" of their actions. The school that decided not to replace the soda machine in case 2 might be thinking precisely that the students broke the machines and therefore the students should experience the "natural consequence" of the action—namely, not being able to buy beverages. Should this common educational idea of a natural consequence be considered a "punishment"? In case 2, the school authority is not directly imposing a hardship; rather, they are allowing a hardship, created by students, to continue. True, they could remove the hardship if they wanted to, but the educators see themselves as not intervening to change the course of events that students have set in motion. Behind the idea of a "natural consequence" is an attempt to remove the element of social authority from the imposition of the negative consequence. Social authority is a key part of the philosophical definition of punishment; so, intentionally or not, allowing a "natural consequence" may be an attempt to remove a response from the category of being a "punishment." When emphasizing the natural consequence, the school hopes that students will come to see that there are reasons for behaving that go beyond the social authority of the educator.

However, while implementation of this strategy attempts to avoid the notion of social control, we should note that there are instances where a "natural consequence" feels very much like a socially sanctioned punishment: to a student who breaks a window and is forced to sit in a cold room, the action *feels like* a hardship imposed by a social authority. Indeed, sometimes allowing a hardship to continue that could be easily removed could be considered intentional imposition of a hardship. Pieper and Pieper summarize this contrarian position on "natural consequences" when they note, in the context of parenting, "When you stand by and let bad things happen, your child experiences the twin disappointments that something went wrong and you did not seem to care enough about her to lift a finger to help prevent the mishap. The 'natural consequences' approach is really a form of punishment."[20] The consequence, in other words, is experienced as an intentionally imposed burden. In addition, we should note that it is not at all clear what is supposed to count as a natural consequence. If a child throws food during lunch, what is the natural consequence? It could be denying lunch to the child the next day, or requiring the child to clean up the mess. Or maybe the natural consequence would be getting food thrown at the child. To our minds, it is not obvious what constitutes the "natural" consequence.

Consider now case 3, the case of removing a student from a situation where excess talking is taking place. An expressive element may or may not be present. Is the teacher expressing a moral disapproval as the consequence is imposed? The student may clearly experience the result as a hardship (as, perhaps, a type of isolation), and the seat change has been imposed by an authority on the occasion of breaking a rule. However, the action may not be intended to imply moral disapproval—it simply allows classroom business to proceed with more order. Therefore, the seat change seems more like a penalty or a sanction, an act of managing the classroom situation through social convention, rather than the sending of a moral message.

Case 4 could have elements of punishment, education, and management. Clearly, when an action endangers oneself and others, there is a strong moral element to the situation. The essay assignment could be seen as a hardship imposed by a social authority to express disapproval of the moral thoughtlessness involved with violating safety procedures. At the same time, writing the essay could be an educational act—the student simply did not know the dangers involved with violating the protocol. Rather than sending the message of moral disapproval, the assignment could be an opportunity to help the student understand the intersection of safety and chemistry. It would be a sort of educational penalty, showing the importance of the classroom convention. The situation, the fire in the classroom, could also be seen as simply a disruption of classroom activities rather than a moral failure, and the essay could be seen as a disincentive to disrupting the classroom in the future. Likely, and perhaps appropriately, the teacher might be considering all three reasons in responding with the essay assignment.

Finally, consider case 5, about the student who is acting out violently. Again, intentions matter, but this seems like an example of "prevention" or "quarantine" rather than punishment. The idea behind the separation is not to send an expressive message to either the student or the community. It may feel like a hardship for the student but will not be perceived that way by many observers. Thus, separating a student for safety reasons might count not as a punishment, per se, but as something else. Still, some of the moral issues associated with punishment (unequal treatment across groups of students, as we will see) remain.

In sum, how we think of punishment and punishment versus discipline seems to depend on a number of interpretations and intentions. These include different understandings of what forms a hardship. There are different interpretations of what constitutes a moral issue and what constitutes a classroom-management issue. The same action could be a simple violation of social convention or be fraught with moral implications, depending on the context. The intention behind the action seems to matter, as does the type of emotional and moral expression that is behind the punitive behavior. The meanings of punishment also seem to fluctuate depending on different notions of social authority in education—who has the authority to punish and what gives them that authority. We hardly need to point out that understandings of these types of issues might change markedly over time, between different contexts and historical epochs, as well. As we will see, one thing we can learn from studying history is how interpretations of hard treatment and social authority have shifted across time. Not every assumption we make about punishment and discipline has been universally shared.

Justifications of Punishment: Retribution, Deterrence, and Reform

Punishment is so common in schools and the larger society that we often simply take its existence for granted. But it is not something that we should so easily accept. It is, after all, the intentional imposition of a harm or hardship on another person. Harming another person should never simply be taken as a matter of course; rather, it is something to rigorously interrogate and continuously reexamine. Critical engagement is even more important in the case of children in schools. The questions are numerous: Are children fully responsible for their actions, and if not, what does that mean for punishment? Is it worth the harm that can occur to the teacher-student relationship? Does it prioritize force and submission to authority instead of the sharing of reasons through open communication—is it anti-educational, in other words? Does it allow teachers to slide by with boring and uninspiring lesson plans, content to rely on punishment when kids get understandably unruly? It is worth considering these questions in some detail.

The justification for punishment, in a general sense, has been hotly debated.[21] Some see the justification of punishment as based in the desirability of future consequences. For example, a punishment might *deter* students' future immoral behavior, or it might *reform* guilty students by communicating to them the moral structure of the world (partly through the "expressive function" of punishment that we have described). These are both possible positive consequences of punishment, occurring in the future. Others see punishment as justified by looking at what is *deserved* for past behavior. If one student harms another, it is simply fair and right that a proportional harm be caused to the guilty student. This is the sentiment behind *retributive* theories of punishment.

It seems to us that both the consequentialist justification and the retributive justification are inadequate when each is considered on its own, and we would favor a mixture of backward- and forward-looking justifications. Consequentialist arguments might justify punishment as a deterrent but in doing so might also justify inflicting a harsh penalty on someone who is merely accused of being guilty. Deterrence works with only the appearance of guilt, which presents a problem for this argument, and a sole focus on deterrence would allow for highly disproportional levels of punishment. For example, imagine that a student is expelled for stealing a teacher's pencil, and that the student is actually innocent and was framed as a violator. The expulsion might be an extremely effective deterrent to future pencil stealing but would obviously be unjust on multiple levels. An innocent person has been punished in the pursuit of deterrence, after all, and the punishment is not proportional to the alleged wrong. Future-looking justifications of deterrence do not tell us why any of this is unjust, since the positive consequence has been achieved. Backward-looking justifications seem necessary to help us see *who* should be punished (namely, only the guilty) and *how much* punishment is justified, given the infraction, even as the punishment is ultimately justified by reference to a desirable future consequence, such as deterrence.[22] Something in addition to deterrence must be in play, then—something that reaches back into the past. In this respect, resources from retributive theories seem essential. The past will tell us who should be punished, and will offer some guidance about how much punishment is justified, given the offense.

Still, retributive justifications alone seem particularly inappropriate in school settings, especially with young children. The idea that a perpetrator deserves a burden simply because of what this person has done in the past assumes a notion of moral responsibility. People deserve punishments, if they do, because they freely chose to do something wrong, violated known social norms, and were aware of future outcomes. That is, they were acting as full moral agents, with the capacity to choose other paths. It is an open question whether anyone is a full moral agent in this sense, but children and youth in schools should clearly not be regarded as such. Their brains are still maturing, and their experiences are limited. They are better classified as *developing* moral agents, who, we should assume, will make many mistakes as they learn to interact with others over time. Someone who lacks moral agency escapes the full claims of retributive justifications (this is precisely the reasoning behind the so-called "insanity defense" in law). Still, there should be some elements of past-looking justifications in school punishment. In schools, it would still be important to punish only the guilty and for punishment to be proportionate to any infractions. These are key ethical requirements in any just community where punishment exists, and preserving these requirements in school would convey to students a part of the moral structure of their social universe.

So, both backward- and forward-looking elements are needed, but what justifications should be emphasized? If punishment is justified in schools, it seems better to focus on deterrence and reform. Certainly, schools have actions that they want to prevent and discourage. They want to prevent misbehavior within the school itself. School personnel want to stop bullying, cheating, harassment, property damage, assault, and behavior that disrupts classroom activities. Schools also want to deter certain actions outside of school and over the life span of a student. Perhaps, as part of their educational mission, they want to discourage things like future drug use and future acts of racism. It seems undeniable that certain forms of punishment and penalty do work to deter certain forms of action in the short term. It is preposterous to claim that the threat of a parking ticket, for example, fails to affect people's parking behavior. Indeed, the threat of parking tickets looms large when deciding where, when, and how to park. We can personally remember threats of being sent to the principal's office or missing recess similarly influencing our own behavior in schools. To say that punishment is an ineffective means of short-term social control is to seem oblivious to these social facts. Still, not every form of punishment deters every form of behavior. It is an open question whether the death penalty deters murder, for example, with the evidence favoring the idea that it does not affect murder rates.[23]

There are times when schools legitimately want to discourage certain behaviors and require an efficient means to do so. In such cases, threats of punishment (in the case of moral action) or penalty (in the case of school conventions) may be justified. But the question for schools that are interested in deterrence becomes fourfold. First, what evidence is there that specific threats of punishment deter specific problematic student behaviors? Second, what evidence is there that punishment is the only way to deter these behaviors (there might be others that are less costly to the teacher-student relationship)? Third, if punishment deters these behaviors, are there any negative consequences to the school-student relationship or the school-community relationship? Fourth, is the punishment likely to be effective at changing moral character and behavior in the long term? It is unlikely that there will be any conclusive evidence concerning many of these questions, of course, but it is nevertheless helpful for those concerned with school order to adopt a reflective stance, engaging directly with these pressing issues.

Beyond deterrence, the idea of reform through punishment is perhaps most at home in education. As we will see, this concept was quite common in the history of schooling. Education, at its best, is about improving our thinking, our values, and our dispositions. The goal, however, is not to "train" students to behave through punitive brainwashing or stimulus-response conditioning. The goal of education is to engage the student as a developing moral agent, send the message that a past action was wrong, help the student understand *why* the action was wrong, and begin the process of inner, voluntary change. The goal is not so much to change behavior but to help students care about moral norms and become responsible moral agents. Under the aim of moral reform, the job of punishment is, as Duff states, "not so much to reform the offender as to persuade offenders that and why they should reform themselves."[24]

The justification for punishment as moral reform connects with ideas in the previous sections about the expressive function: there may be times when rational educational techniques, like talking things through, are not enough to communicate the moral significance of what a student has done, in the eyes of the student, the school, and the community. A punishment may be necessary to educate everyone about the seriousness of the action and the seriousness of the response and for the offender to express true remorse. Duff's idea that punishment plays a role in the communication of moral norms in a way that words alone cannot, and that it allows the community to express its emotional response and the offender an opportunity to express remorse, is the most convincing justification for punishment. Indeed, we believe that this argument vindicates the thoughtful use of punishment in schools. Under certain circumstances, punishment might indeed play a role in the expression of morality and in rebuilding relationships, and this might allow for individual reform and moral education. Here again, though, educators need to ask whether the reforming message of a *particular* punishment has the effects that are intended over the long term, or whether it simply engenders resentment and loathing. We will talk about some particular pitfalls a bit later.

Criticisms of Punishment in Schools, and Some Responses

For now, we can also approach the question from the opposite direction and examine the concerns that have been raised against the use of punishment in schools. There are several reasons given for why punishment has no role to play in education. First, we have discussed punishment as involving issues of morality (as opposed to classroom discipline, which is about social efficiency). Some consider morality a private matter, however, and are therefore uncomfortable with schools as a public entity taking a moral stand through punishment.[25] The idea is that public institutions should remain neutral in conversations about disputed questions, like those involved with human morality. With punishment, however, schools take a side where they should remain quiet. Second, some have argued that punishment is ineffective at improving behavior or teaching about right and wrong.[26] Critics of punishment often point to classic behavioral studies, sometimes involving animals, that show punishment is ineffective at producing long-term behavioral change. When the threat of punishment is removed, the previous behavior returns.[27] Third, punishment could be seen as authoritarian and therefore fundamentally opposed to educational ideals. Education should help students learn to act based on good reasons, not because a stronger adult threatens punishment. Fourth, punishment is sometimes used as a cover for poor instruction or ineffective classroom-management practices. Educator A. S. Neill makes this point in a heavy-handed way: "Thousands of teachers do their work splendidly without having to introduce fear of punishment. The others are incompetent misfits who ought to be driven out of the profession."[28]

There is something important to all of these arguments. Collectively and separately, they should give educators serious pause when thinking about punishment. For example, it is certainly the case that poorly run schools and classrooms breed student "misbehavior." As R. S. Peters notes, "An experienced teacher knows well enough the sorts of incidents that are likely to promote disorder and will anticipate and avoid them. Under normal conditions enthusiasm for the enterprise, combined with imaginative techniques of presentation and efficient class management will avert the need for punishment."[29] Indeed, students who are bored, condescended to, and demeaned within school environments are likely to "act out" in ways the school does not like. Students who attend classes in crumbling school buildings are unlikely to put much stock in the idea that a school and its rules are worth much attention. Students who see that schoolwork offers little help with the problems they confront on a daily basis or that it does little to improve the lives of others in their neighborhoods are not likely to think of school rules as being relevant and significant. Thus, schools resorting to tough discipline and punishment policies should reflect on how their own teaching practices and school environments may contribute to student misbehavior.[30]

There is also something to the criticisms that schools should be in the business of building reasoning skills and that punishment might work against that development. Punishment is an act of force undertaken by a social authority. If schools are concerned about student behavior and if they take the development of reason seriously, they should give reasons and try to persuade their students, not impose conformity by brute force. Education writer Alfie Kohn argues that whatever messages we send to children by punishing them, they are not the sort conducive to a genuine moral life. The ideas that children receive from punishment are ideas about adult power. Children do not think about what they did wrong, they think about how to escape punishment the next time; they do not feel remorse, they feel anger and resentment; and they do not consider the others they harmed, they think of their own pain at being punished. Instead of promoting moral reflection, then, punishment in schools distracts children from key moral issues, makes them angry, and makes them more self-centered. Kohn states, "When we punish, in other words, we lead children to ask, 'What do they (the grown-ups with the power) want me to do, and what will happen to me if I don't do it?' This is very different from the sort of question we want children to ask themselves, 'What kind of person do I want to be?'"[31] Punishment centers students' thoughts on what their actions mean for themselves, not on those that their actions affect. This is particularly true if schools are thinking of punishment as a way of teaching the public morality of respecting others as equals. In that case, we want these values internalized so that they manifest themselves outside of an environment of school social control. This happens when students understand and "buy in" to these values. Punishment by itself is unsuccessful in promoting the sort of social reasoning and moral values that we want to instill.

In the face of these serious questions about punishment, how might a defender of punishment in schools respond? The first objection was that school punishment inappropriately involves the state in matters of personal morality. This is a valid issue. It may indeed be inappropriate for schools to punish students for, say, engaging in consensual sexual relations (although attitudes around this have ebbed and flowed historically).[32] At the same time, it is impossible for schools to avoid value judgments and to be neutral with respect to controversial visions of the human good. The choice of a curriculum, the structure of classrooms, and so forth all reflect value judgments about good and bad, right and wrong. Some connection with contested moral issues will be unavoidable in schools. Furthermore, there does exist a notion of public morality that undergirds life in liberal-democratic societies. These public moral values include a respect for persons and, with that, a belief in freedom, justice, and equality. Schools, then, can take a stand on things like the immorality of racism without violating a realm of private conscience. And, as a corollary of these values, students cannot make other students feel unsafe or disrupt their learning, not simply for the sake of efficiency but also for the sake of showing respect. Schools can and should take steps to support these values through education into the public morality. As long as punishment focuses on public morality, on just social relations, it will be on strong political footing. One of the problems with contemporary approaches to punishment, as we will see, is the moral vacuum that schools seem to operate in. A proper understanding of discipline and punishment in schools will involve gaining a clearer conception of the moral communities that schools should be.

What could an educator say to the objection that punishment is simply a cover for poor teaching? It is true that any teacher who is tempted to punish needs to consider what factors in the school environment may have contributed to the situation—in fact, this will be a key point for our analysis moving forward. At the same time, we should not go to the other extreme and argue that schools are completely responsible for student behavior. School practices are vitally important, to be sure, but students have lives outside of school that impact their behavior within school. Behavior patterns are often established and reinforced at home, in the community, or in the media. If a student comes to school under the influence of drugs or alcohol and acts in an unruly manner, for example, it is unclear whether even the best classroom-management practices could effectively counter that situation. Such cases might be rare, but they do exist. More commonly, the realities of overcrowded and under-resourced classrooms push against ideal teaching practices. A misbehaving student might be brought around through the sustained attention of caring teachers, but this is not always possible given classroom realities.

Whether punishment is, by nature, authoritarian and anti-educational is perhaps one of the most interesting and pressing questions because it strikes at the heart of the educational project. Can punishment play any sort of role in developing ethical behavior and moral reasoning? The research of behavioral psychologists seems to indicate that, at least under the narrow punishment conditions associated with their studies, negative behaviors return immediately after exterior punishment is removed. Negative behavior is only temporarily suppressed, a view that is supported by recent research on corporal punishment.[33] Punishment is therefore thought to be ineffective at changing deep attitudes and long-term behaviors. Of course, this conclusion is mostly based on research with animals or with simple punishment situations, like corporal punishments, not on complex discursive contexts where the punishment is also surrounded by reason giving, caring relationships, and community responses. Think of the kinds of complex dialogic exchanges involving punishment that are imagined by Duff. Punishment becomes a mode of communication between individuals and communities. There are many different types of punishment beyond electric shocks and denying food pellets to rats, and different punishments would likely have different roles and show different effects.

Critics like Kohn imagine students having conversations in their heads during punishment that center on their own resentment and their plans about avoiding punishment in the future. This sort of thing makes it hard for critics to see how authentic moral attitudes can emerge from punishment. However, we can also imagine other thoughts children might have, not simply those envisioned by Kohn. To the extent that Kohn's imagined conversations do occur in the minds of students, we can also picture how they might be counteracted and disrupted by thoughtful educators. Schools would need to pair punishment with other sorts of activities that do promote reflection on and engagement with the moral questions that a student's behavior has presented. These exercises would need to counter the anger, resentment, and self-centeredness that often arise when a student is punished. But a critic might ask, Why not just focus on these discursive activities rather than on punishment? As we have seen, a process of dialogue and apology is insufficient to communicate the moral significance of some harms, both to the perpetrator and to the community. Punishment can play a role in the development of moral reason by clarifying the voice of the community (saying, "This action *really matters to us*") in a way that words alone cannot, thus allowing for a certain sort of communicative exchange. Punishment can also play a role in restoring relationships if a student comes to accept a punishment and, in so doing, makes a statement to the community about a desire to reintegrate. The division between punishment, then, and dialogic reasoning is a false dichotomy. While punishment *alone* is insufficient in the enterprise of moral education and indeed may be counterproductive, it seems to have a place in these activities when used thoughtfully and judiciously. To suggest that there might be some role for punishment in education is not, of course, to defend all types of punishment. We now turn to some specific types of punishment that seem particularly problematic.

Some Key Ethical Issues in School Punishment

We have explored the conceptual and justificatory issues involved with punishment, with a focus on understanding some concerns with school punishment. We have suggested that the expressive function of punishment and the conversations that punishment makes possible plausibly give punishment a valid role to play in education. Along the way, we have pointed to various preliminary questions to consider when constructing and implementing policies around discipline. Punishment must be surrounded by a context of moral reflection and ongoing dialogue. There are, however, some topics that deserve sustained attention because of their persistence over time or because of their newfound relevance to contemporary educational policy. In what follows, we sketch these issues, highlighting some recent research, pointing out some ethical dimensions, and setting the stage for more extended treatment in the succeeding chapters.

The ethical issue currently getting the most attention when it comes to punishment, and deservedly so, is the unequal treatment of different social groups. The empirical data is clear: Black students are much more likely to be punished in US P–12 schools (i.e., preschool through twelfth grade) than White students. A study from the US Government Accountability Office (GAO) found that Black students account for 15.5 percent of all students enrolled in public school but 39 percent of all students suspended from school. The GAO also found that this disparity holds true across all types of schools and, importantly, across all types of income levels. Disparities also exist between boys and girls. Boys constitute 51 percent of the student population but account for 70 percent of the suspensions—although intersectionality of race and gender is important here: Black girls are suspended six times as often as White girls.[34] Students with disabilities are also overrepresented in the group of punished students, by 13.2 percent. These differences between groups are troubling to those with egalitarian ideals and suggest some sort of bias is at work. The report carefully notes that disparities in student discipline "taken alone, do not establish whether unlawful discrimination has occurred."[35]

A second ethical issue has to do with the widespread use of "exclusionary" punishment. The most common forms of exclusionary punishment are suspension and expulsion, both of which remove students from the school environment. Data from the National Center for Education Statistics (NCES) show that in 2013–2014, 5.3 percent of all students in US public schools received a suspension. Boys were suspended at a far higher rate (7.3 percent) than girls (3.2 percent). In the same year, 111,000 students were reportedly expelled, or about 0.2 percent of US public school students.[36] It is understandable that educators, who are often faced with inadequate resources and large classes, might want to remove disruptive students, and even more so when a student has been behaving violently toward other students or teachers. Still, the effects of exclusionary punishment are quite negative. Summarizing the totality of the evidence on the long-term effects of suspensions and expulsions, the American Academy of Pediatrics states,

> The adverse effects of out-of-school suspension and expulsion on the student can be profound. The student is separated from the educational process, and the school district may not be obligated to provide any further educational or counseling services for the student. Data suggest that students who are involved in the juvenile justice system are likely to have been suspended or expelled. Further, students who experience out-of-school suspension and expulsion are as much as 10 times more likely to ultimately drop out of high school than are those who do not. The student who does not complete high school can expect to earn considerably less over a working career and to have far fewer educational and employment opportunities from which to choose than a student who has completed high school. If the student's parent(s) work, there may be no one at home during the day to supervise the student's activity, making it more likely that the student (1) will not pursue a home-based education program; (2) will engage in more inappropriate behavior; and (3) will associate with other individuals who will further increase the aforementioned risks.[37]

A later study by Johanna Lacoe and Matthew Steinberg, looking at the effects of changing policies surrounding suspension in Philadelphia schools, supported many of these findings. Suspension decreased math and reading performance for those students who were suspended. Importantly, the study also looked at whether suspension benefited students who were not suspended, those who remained in school. After all, it could be argued that while suspension may hurt the student who leaves, it benefits those who remain. The authors report, "Our findings do not support the claim that greater exposure to suspensions via the removal of students from school through out-of-school suspension benefits peers. Indeed, exposure to suspensions for more serious infractions is related to declines in peer achievement, though these estimates are modest."[38]

The harms of exclusionary punishment are compounded when they are focused on certain racial groups. The "discipline gap," the differences between groups when it comes to receiving suspensions and expulsions, is widely considered to be a factor in the "achievement gap," the differences between groups in terms of academic success. One group of researchers, looking at the available evidence, concluded that "disproportionate school discipline experienced by some racial and ethnic groups has important implications for academic outcomes."[39] This has been confirmed by more recent research. In one large-scale study in Kentucky, researchers found that schools with a higher population of Black students used exclusionary punishment more frequently. Overall, Black and Latino students were at increased risk of being suspended compared to students from other racial groups. This made a significant impact on the students' school performance. The researchers found that suspended students' math and reading test scores at the end of the year were significantly behind the scores of those who were not suspended. Also, students who were likely to be suspended scored lower in the years they were suspended than in the years that they were not. The authors estimate that school suspensions account for roughly one-fifth of the Black-White achievement gap. Since Black students are suspended at a far higher rate than White students, the uptake is that Black students are disproportionately harmed by this particular type of punishment practice.[40]

The NCES data captures this racial disparity on a larger scale. In the year 2013–2014, 13.7 percent of Black students received an out-of-school suspension, compared to 3.4 percent of White students, 4.5 percent of Hispanic students, 1.1 percent of Asian students, 4.5 percent of Pacific Islander students, and 6.7 percent of American Indian students. The percentage of Black and American Indian students that were expelled from school (roughly 0.4 percent) was nearly double the percentage of all other groups (roughly 0.2 percent).[41]

Why should society be concerned about this as a matter of justice? Exclusionary punishments seek to temporarily or permanently separate students from the school environment. The idea is that students who allegedly misbehave must be removed from classrooms, both as a warning and deterrent to them and as a way of protecting classroom order and learning. We will be arguing against this practice throughout the book. For now, we will simply say that, as the Academy of Pediatrics notes, exclusionary punishments do lasting harm to students by placing them significantly behind other students, leading to additional problems inside and outside of school and endangering their future flourishing. Exclusion weakens feelings of connection that students might otherwise have toward the school environment and toward the public sphere more broadly. Recall the idea that punishment has an expressive function, one that sends the message of moral disapproval. There are also secondary expressions tied to punishments that relate to the specific punishment practice. The secondary expressions of exclusionary punishment unavoidably send the message that a student's presence is not welcome, that the student has nothing to offer or contribute, that school is not appropriate for this person.

Less common, but still divisive and ethically fraught, is the use of corporal punishment, our third ethical issue. Corporal punishment is still a widely accepted form of punishment in the United States. A 2014 poll found that 49 percent of Americans agree that corporal punishment can be an effective way to teach children right from wrong. In addition, 81 percent think spanking should be legal as long as it does not cause significant physical damage.[42] It is legal for schools to administer corporal punishment in nineteen states, and corporal punishment is banned in thirty-one states. The most common form of such punishment in schools is paddling. In 2011–2012, 163,333 students were reported to have been subject to corporal punishment.[43] As with other forms of punishment, male students, students with disabilities, and Black students receive corporal punishment at higher rates than other groups.[44] Black students, in fact, are 51 percent more likely to be physically punished than White students in the states where corporal punishment is most widespread.[45] Yet the practice of corporal punishment is slowly declining. Once widespread, corporal punishment was practiced in 2013–2014 by only 3 percent of American schools (approximately 4,000 out of 132,853). The reasons for the shift away from corporal punishment are part of a story that will be told in subsequent chapters, and are linked to the rise of managerial systems of school control.[46] We will also explore the ethical status of corporal punishment by investigating the harms that it causes and the secondary expressions associated with it.

Conclusion

In this survey of school punishment, our purpose was to introduce some central concepts, major arguments, and pressing issues. One of the central features of the concept of punishment is that it has an "expressive function," in that it sends a message of moral disapproval. This makes punishment different from sanctions, penalties, and other disciplining practices. Punishment should be used when students violate moral norms, while disciplining strategies should be used for violations of school convention. The burden imposed by punishment can make the communication of disapproval "symbolically adequate" to the moral offense, allowing for certain conversations to take place. It provides the moral community with a powerful voice of disapproval, to be sure, while also providing the offending student with a chance to show remorse and apologize with a greater depth of meaning. This dialogic process gives punishment a legitimate place in schools, we believe, when punishment is used with wisdom, discernment, and constraint. At the same time, we should recognize punishment practices that are ethically problematic—in particular, the racial disparities in punishment and the associated school-to-prison pipeline, the widespread use of exclusionary punishment, and corporal punishment. Punishment has an expressive function, yes, but particular forms of punishment have secondary expressions that send their own messages, and many of these messages are harmful from an educational perspective. We track all of these ideas throughout the chapters that follow.

Punishment in Early American Schools

The United States is a young country, both in its recent establishment and, for much of its history, in its demographic makeup.[1] The American population's youth and mobility made education integral to the national project; it would be a means of imposing social order and cohesion on a disparate public with few institutions of centralized authority. So much more, then, did schools themselves need to exercise control: in early America, public freedom became intrinsically bound up with children's education and schools' methods of constraining and punishing misbehavior. Order was the goal, but punishment was never simply a means of keeping classrooms quiet. Instead, its aim was the formation of independent citizens, an undertaking inseparable from other forms of political education. The schoolroom would assume outsize significance in colonies organized around piety and commerce, as well as in an emerging democratic-republican state. The ways in which schools disciplined children pointed to the sorts of individuals that those children were expected to become. Whether or not teachers and students realized it, the daily round of classroom mischief and correction unavoidably tested prevailing theories of self-government, as well as the questions of social authority, personal agency, and human relationships raised in the previous chapter.

In the following sections, we outline three types of discipline and punishment that American educators relied on between the seventeenth and nineteenth centuries and explain the political, cultural, and philosophical contexts that ascribed them legitimacy. First, we discuss corporal punishment, which derived from authoritarian or patriarchal worldviews and focused on pain as a means of subordination. Next, drawing from liberal political and economic theories, we discuss shame, which encouraged the internalization of discipline through a series of decentralized interactions with peers. Finally, we discuss moral suasion, a Romantic approach that relied on emotional norms to elicit good behavior. Each of these methods had shortcomings, yet we do not present them simply to dismiss them out of hand nor to cast their adherents as inherently cruel or benighted. Use of corporal punishment, shame, and moral suasion arose at particular times (and continues today) because they addressed problems of classroom order and moral development in ways that were more or less consistent and understandable to large swaths of the population. Thus, while subsequent chapters will present compelling arguments for our own conception of just punishment, it is important to acknowledge that reasonable people could support earlier systems as well.

That the moral foundations for these punishments were easily apprehensible and largely unchanging, however, should also remind us that adherents of each have existed throughout American history, with their cultural prominence rising or falling based on concerns of the moment. School punishment has always been contested and always in flux; it was never as totalizing as one might expect. Thus, the real purpose of this chapter is to ensure that readers gain a nuanced understanding of the issue as an ongoing debate, so that those who persist in support for earlier methods of punishment do so honestly, without relying on nostalgia or oversimplifications. An examination of past practices is helpful only insofar as it brings difficult disciplinary decisions to life. To endorse a punishment simply on the basis of tradition or visions of a simpler past—or worse, to proceed without any consideration of its previous iterations—is to squander the lessons of history.

Amid ongoing discussions of self-government, readers should also remember that constructions of citizenship are often exclusionary, establishing a political community by subordinating or distancing those outside of it. In this case, the expansion of suffrage during the early nineteenth century applied questions of education and punishment primarily to White boys and—although they were generally unable to vote or hold property—to White girls, who gained access to education through their status as the mothers of future citizens. For much of the nineteenth century, in the North, South, and West of the United States, non-White children faced neglect, segregation, and forced exclusion from formal schooling as means of denying them social or political equality. Indeed, the public lands that endowed many states' educational systems came from the expropriation of Indigenous peoples' territory, while the system of chattel slavery relied on an outright prohibition of literacy among enslaved people. By the 1860s, racial and ethnic minorities had overcome significant obstacles to secure access for their children, but the systematic denial of educational opportunity made them latecomers to debates over school discipline. Thus, while we will briefly discuss how racist ideologies informed

punishment of non-White students during the nineteenth century, more substantive discussion of racial and economic inequalities will appear in chapter 3,
and readers should assume that most of the children described in this chapter
are White, unless otherwise noted.

Authoritarianism and Corporal Punishment

Corporal punishment, which for our purposes refers to any infliction of physical pain or discomfort on a student, was a nearly universal practice in American schools from the seventeenth century to the nineteenth century, and it
remains prevalent in some regions of the country today. Most subsequent
forms of punishment emerged in opposition to it, and as such it remains a
touchstone for any history of school discipline. What were its origins, and
why did so many Americans believe in its efficacy?

It is important to note, first, that while corporal punishment may seem like
a natural or timeless response to childhood misbehavior—present in schools
since antiquity and a common child-rearing technique in the home—it was
nevertheless a culturally specific phenomenon.[2] Native Americans were far
less punitive toward their children than Europeans were: they refused to whip
them and "only reproved [them] with gentle words." This disparity troubled
European colonizers, who worried that their own children might defect to
the natives and "succumb to the savagery of the forest world that surrounded
them." Their fears had some basis in reality. Children captured by Native
Americans often refused to return home, finding Indigenous life preferable
to the colonial regimen of work, church, and school, all of which imparted
values through the threat of physical force.[3]

Corporal punishment was central to the Calvinist theology preached in
Puritan New England and in Presbyterian communities farther south. It ultimately disseminated through most evangelical denominations, which coun-
seled stern responses to human depravity, mortification of the flesh for spiritual benefit, and the maintenance of order through patriarchy, with the teacher
acting in place of the father and the father in place of God. Proponents cited
Old Testament passages to justify whipping in schools, such as "Foolishness
is bound up in the heart of a child but the rod of correction shall drive it far
from him."[4] Because impulsive behavior was interpreted as a manifestation of
original sin, physical punishment became the means to break children's will
and bring them into accordance with divine authority. "There is in all children," wrote John Robinson of Plymouth, Massachusetts, "a stubbornness,
and stoutness of mind arising from natural pride, which must, in the first
place, be broken and beaten down."[5] In 1645, the civic leaders of Dorchester,

Massachusetts, decreed, "Because the Rodd of Correction is an ordinance of God necessary sometymes to bee dispenced unto Children . . . , [it] is therefore ordered and agreed that the schoolmaster for the tyme beeing shall haue full power to minister correction to all or any of his schollers."[6] Fifty years later, the Reverend Cotton Mather exhorted parents to "curb, check, [and] correct . . . your ungodly children. Better they be whipped than damned."[7] Onward through the eighteenth and nineteenth centuries, teachers continued, on biblical authority, to cite domination and pain as the only forces that students would respect. "The fundamental motive of obedience is *fear*," wrote Hubbard Winslow in 1834. "Other powerful motives operate, but all are ultimately *sustained* by this. Take this away, and all other motives lose their efficacy. Hence the first practical lesson for children is, that transgression is followed by punishment. If they *sin*, they will *suffer*."[8]

Such statements typify the religious rhetoric of punishment through much of American history, but it is easy to misinterpret their relationship to disciplinary practice. For one thing, they suggest a severity that did not extend to all parents or teachers. Puritans were also beneficiaries of the first wave of parenting literature, which proliferated among European Lutherans in the late sixteenth century. These texts seated discipline firmly in the hands of fathers, whom they saw as less pliable than mothers, but while they cautioned that "too little discipline was more harmful than too much" and that a loving parent did not shirk from physical correction, they also encouraged sensitivity to each child's disposition and level of reason. Most of all, they stressed that punishment should be "coolly" applied, and that fathers were not "hangmen."[9] In the same vein, notes historian Steven Mintz, Puritan authorities "were highly critical of harsh physical punishments." They admonished parents "always to explain the reasons for a punishment" and "never to discipline a child in anger." Indeed, the Puritans were the first to pass laws *limiting* the father's ability to beat his children and were as likely to criticize parents for laxity or brutality as they were children for defiance. The same moral framework provided at least general guidance for teachers who reached for the rod.[10]

Reliance on sermons and religious proclamations as evidence of historical punishment also overlooks the public response to official orthodoxies. For example, after bestowing on schoolmasters the right to strike children, the city of Dorchester, Massachusetts, ordered that "no parent or other of the Inhabitants shall hinder or goe about to hinder the master" in doing so, which suggests there was at least latent resistance to the law. One can find numerous other cases in which individual parents shirked their responsibilities to impose strict discipline or openly defied authorities who did so.[11] Thus, the religious origins of corporal punishment were somewhat less encompassing than one might assume, and fixation on the subject by Puritans and their successors may speak more to their insecurities about social change and civil authority than to the realities of school punishment. That is, their endorsements should be taken as prescriptions of an ideological ideal rather than descriptions of actual practices.[12]

Children were whipped in school, but the act is better understood in terms of folk culture—part of a premodern sensibility with shorter and less cosseted visions of childhood—which often rejected the sanctimony of Puritan leaders but accepted their basic equation of authority with physical domination. For many parents, pain and the threat of force were prerequisites for order, no less in the era's schools than in its families and local communities, and it was the nexus between these three institutions that formed the real basis for corporal punishment.

The United States was a patriarchal society, and most of its inhabitants lived in some state of unfreedom through the middle of the nineteenth century. Enslaved people, women, indentured servants, apprentices, imprisoned people, soldiers, and sailors were all bound in one way or another, and all could be whipped by their superiors for minor infractions. Many towns demonstrated the expressive function of punishment by maintaining posts and pillories for public floggings, which (proponents claimed) satisfied public demands for justice and deterred others from committing crimes. Schoolchildren were subject to the same treatment under the common-law principle of in loco parentis, in which public authorities acted in place of the parent. At least one school, in Sunderland, Massachusetts, had a whipping post in the middle of the classroom, to which children could be tied and beaten in front of their classmates.[13] Schools themselves were organized to support local economic and political structures, in ways that practically necessitated corporal punishment. Provisions for education differed by region—from tax-supported schools in Northern towns to schools funded by a mixture of taxes and "rate bills" in rural areas to privately funded (or simply nonexistent) schools in most parts of the South—but low costs and decentralized governance were the rule everywhere. In most cases, classes were held in one-room buildings that were overcrowded and disorganized, with sporadic attendance and students of a wide range of ages and abilities, governed by a single male teacher with no formal training. In their infliction of pain and their adherence to obedience and submission, then, schools were in step with the largely agrarian society around them: deference to authority was more important than academic skills, and affordable costs were more important still.[14]

Nevertheless, the consensus around corporal punishment was regularly renegotiated. Punishment relied on shifting standards of consent and social legitimacy, and although teachers administered beatings with blanket invocations of in loco parentis, parents themselves often criticized the practice, both individually and in groups.[15] In a typical case, from 1780, Boston selectmen had to suspend two children from school after their father punched a teacher who had struck them. In this case, the selectmen were unsympathetic to complaints about teacher brutality, reminding parents "of the mischief which might follow from any weakening of the *government* of the public schools," and encouraging the teachers to "continue [their] best endeavors to maintain . . . order."[16] But charges of child abuse did not only come from individual families. At times such charges became a means to assert parental prerogative writ large and to check the rising power of teachers and school boards. One finds waves of abuse allegations with the transition from home tutorials to pay schools in the late eighteenth century, and more with the emergence of publicly funded common schools in the mid-nineteenth century. Corporal punishment became a signal question amid rapidly changing educational norms. At issue in these cases was not whether children should be physically punished at all but whether it was the parent's or the teacher's right to do so, and whether by inflicting punishment a public authority was intruding into the privacy of the family (a concern that, as we saw in the previous chapter, continues today in debates about whether public schools should take moral positions). Complaints about school discipline could provide leverage in other political disputes as well, as local factions denounced harsh teachers to check or unseat their supporters on the school board. All this is to say that despite widespread support, corporal punishment was politicized from the very beginning and often became a stand-in for broader debates about schools, families, and the exercise of power, with children's bodies emerging as the site of struggle.[17]

It is important to note that those bodies were not passive objects, that the premodern mindset did not guarantee or even expect students' acquiescence to whippings, and that the legitimacy of punishment was subject to ongoing scrutiny from children too. Corporal punishment made explicit the contest for power in the classroom, and children, imitating the riotous atmosphere of the era's street politics, became "violent little partisans" in defense of their rights.[18] Students routinely turned out teachers they deemed overly punitive and barricaded the schoolhouse door to prevent reentry. Older boys sometimes subdued teachers and meted out their own punishments, occasionally killing their instructors. After a teacher punched one of their classmates and beat another bloody, students at a New Hampshire school "ripped the ruler from his grasp, hauled him outside, and threw him down an icy hillside." Another teacher had his head thrust into a stove, which singed off his eyebrows. A third was hog-tied and left in the schoolhouse while the children went home.[19] Numerous stories feature boys sneaking up behind their teachers and walloping them with log chains.[20] Boys in Baltimore, after throwing inkstands at their teacher, marveled that anyone would take a job with "so many wounds, cuts and bruises."[21] By the end of the nineteenth century, teaching manuals explicitly acknowledged students' ability to condone or reject systems of punishment based on their own notions of fairness, and warned the novice teacher not to punish too many of the children, lest he "cause sympathy of numbers to go against him and side with those who have been punished."[22] Student uprisings, like parent protests, had the potential to moderate classroom punishments according to standards of folk practice. There is, perhaps, something in this system of checks and balances that holds lessons for educators today. While teachers of the past were certainly socially sanctioned authorities, the threat of resistance introduced a notion of accountability for punishment and gave the teacher-student relationship a semblance of moral equality. Teachers were forced to engage with students' senses of right and wrong, fairness and unfairness, at least on a minimal level. Although their actions were supported by moral codes and public opinion, teachers recognized that they were nevertheless open to challenge, a form of public scrutiny. This idea of punishment being open to challenge will play a part in our own views of appropriate forms of punishment.

Thus far, we have discussed both the ideological foundations of corporal punishment and some of the forces that restrained it. If restive students disturbed classroom order, on one hand, or if punishments were too harsh or high-handed, on the other, parents became dissatisfied and fired the teacher. These competing imperatives were colorfully illustrated in Leadville, Colorado, in the 1880s, when the board of education at first struggled to fill a teaching vacancy "because none of the applicants was tough enough" but eventually had to dismiss its selected candidate for shooting at the students. Within those loose boundaries of acceptable behavior, the public's call for order sanctioned harsh discipline and gave teachers significant discretion in its exercise. (Another Colorado teacher quieted students by firing a pistol at a moose head at the rear of the room. He seems to have kept his job.) Having established a general context for the support of corporal punishment, then, we now turn to the lived realities of its implementation.[23]

It is difficult to know how individual teachers administered corporal punishment or how individual children experienced it. Public discussions of the issue were often clouded with euphemism and nostalgia. In the nineteenth-century

South, people taunted children on their way to class by calling them "school butter," because, like heavy cream, they were about to be whipped.[24] In North Carolina, whippings were referred to as getting an "essence of peach." Adults nationwide still make joking references about "applying the board of education to the seat of knowledge."[25] Such phrases use humor and misdirection to obscure the act itself, softening personal memories and opening the door to moral or ideological sanction through the abstraction of physical pain. This is an impediment to honest deliberation. However one makes sense of corporal punishment, and whatever one's final judgment of its necessity, a true evaluation must confront the phenomenon head on and not rely on received wisdom or conventionality.

Unfortunately, representations in popular culture, particularly in literature and art, are similarly stylized. The stock image of a pre-twentieth-century classroom features a schoolmaster with a wooden switch in his hand, threatening or striking a misbehaving pupil. These depictions generally fall into two types. The first is wry or quaint, presenting the student as a scamp who deserves what he gets but whose spirit remains unbowed. In such scenes, the child's inner strength negates the punishment and renders the teacher impotent. A typical example comes from *The Adventures of Tom Sawyer* (1876), in which the hero is whipped twice, first for talking to Huckleberry Finn, the village ne'er-do-well, and then for claiming responsibility for a torn book. Tom instigates these punishments for his own reasons and responds to them with equanimity. The teacher claims no power over him, and there is no pretense of repentance or moral reform. Likewise, in *The Legend of Sleepy Hollow* (1820), one recognizes Ichabod Crane as a well-meaning but weak character the moment he is introduced as a schoolteacher. Unlike the other men of the town, he gives singing lessons, helps with housework, and tries to whip children judiciously. The "mere puny stripling, that winced at the least flourish of the rod, was passed by with indulgence; but the claims of justice were satisfied by inflicting a double portion on some little tough wrong-headed, broadskirted Dutch urchin, who sulked and swelled and grew dogged and sullen beneath the birch." It is the latter kind of boy, in the form of Brom Van Brunt, who soon drives Ichabod out of town.[26] The second portrayal of corporal punishment is tender and Romantic, contrasting innocent children with tyrannical teachers. One of Walt Whitman's first publications, "Death in the School-Room," features a sickly boy falsely accused of stealing melons. Given an hour's reprieve by his teacher, the boy walks to his desk and quietly dies of a heart condition. The teacher, thinking the boy is asleep, begins to beat him with a rattan switch. Only after a few minutes does he realize, aghast, that he is striking a corpse.[27]

If such scenes emphasize the emotional responses to beatings—ranging from pride to macabre horror—a focus on their physical effects imparts a different set of lessons. Despite common literary portrayals, teachers did not confine themselves to wooden switches or paddles. They were as likely to use ropes, belts, rulers, pointers, hoses, shoes, shingles, books, or whips to strike their pupils; to grab, shove, or slap them; and to pinch their arms, pull their hair, box their ears, or hit them with a thimble on a string. A South Carolinian remembered his teacher flogging a child "until the youngster vomited or wet his breeches," a memory that was far from unique during this period.[28] Many teachers developed techniques that did not leave marks, forcing students to kneel on a wooden wedge with their weight pushing against the point or to stand precariously on stools for extended periods of time. "Some were compelled to hold out, at arm's length, the largest book which could be found, or a great leaden inkstand, till muscle and nerve, bone and marrow, were tortured with the continued exertion," recalled one boy. "I well recollect that one poor fellow forgot his suffering by fainting quite away." Others testified that classmates would be forced to bend, with their fingers on the floor, until the blood rushed to their heads and they fell over. If children whispered, they could have a large wood chip forced between their teeth, painfully prying their jaws open.[29] If they dozed off, they could be made to wear "a necklace of sharp Jamestown weed-burrs, strung on tape."[30] These examples speak to the sadistic imagination with which teachers secured compliance, and blur distinctions between schoolroom punishment and outright torture. If some students bore their beatings with the resolve of Tom Sawyer, plenty of teachers acted like Whitman's gothic tyrant.[31]

Whipping was unjust not merely in its severity but also in the reasons for its application. Teachers sometimes subjected students to collective punishment, beating the entire class to ensure that, "though some of the innocent may have suffered . . . none of the guilty escaped." In a misguided attempt to leverage peer pressure, they also whipped children for others' failure to learn. Massachusetts minister John Barnard remembered being subject to such treatment as a boy, made worse when a classmate intentionally flubbed his recitations. Barnard was beaten for several days running, until he took matters into his own hands and administered "a severe flogging to the [malingering] classmate" after school.[32] Barnard's case may have been an outlier, but it was not uncommon to punish students for wrong answers, which some teachers interpreted as a form of obstinacy. Many critics at the time observed that beating a child who is "willing enough to learn, but whose intelligence is defective, is worse than madness," but the practice persisted until the early twentieth century. Teachers also struck pupils for speaking in languages other than English, for speaking with lisps or stutters, for daydreaming, and for taking alternate approaches to grammar or math problems.[33] These are merely some of the cases in which the primary expression of punishment—moral condemnation—gave way to teachers' frustrations. Whether or not whipping changed children's behavior, it was obviously unjust to punish them for involuntary actions or inaptitude. Strictly speaking, it was not punishment at all.

Even when limited to misbehavior, corporal punishment exacted a toll on students' learning. Students naturally focused not on their lessons but on the sword of Damocles hanging over their heads. As a Puritan writer noted, while a teacher might produce "a number of good Scholars," he often "marred by his severity more than he hath made"; "the *ordinary* Schoolmaster's tyrannical beating and dispiriting of children" was a trauma from which "many tender ingeniose children doe never recover again."[34] William Ellery Channing, who went on to champion gentler means of discipline during the nineteenth century, remembered the terror of seeing the "long round stick" leaning against his teacher's chair like a "watchful, sleepless being of ancient mythology." Another student shuddered thinking about a small ladder by the schoolmaster's desk that he had to climb to receive his beatings.[35] "What's the use of going to *school,*" a boy wondered. "You'll have to sit so still and prim, and learn such hard lessons, and if you dare to open your mouth, won't you catch it!"[36] Meanwhile, from the teacher's perspective, enforcing an authoritarian classroom quickly became an end unto itself, with "half the time spent in calling up scholars for little misdemeanors, trying to make them confess their faults and promise stricter obedience, or in devising punishments and inflicting them."[37] If classroom functions depended on external authority, and especially if the teacher had to safeguard his pride and dignity to retain power, the school day could devolve into a litany of petty transgressions and perceived slights.

Conceiving of punishment as a battle of wills tended to inflame teachers' cruelty. While supporters of corporal punishment insisted that a good teacher would have the breadth to administer it dispassionately—to "smite with the same candor and earnest desire to do good that actuated him while reading the morning lesson from the Bible"—evidence attests to more heated confrontations and even outright sadism.[38] Many children spoke of instructors who derived "morbid pleasure" from beatings. Indeed, some teachers recognized "emotions of doubtful character" within themselves.[39] A boy in Massachusetts, when asked why he quit school, responded, "The teacher whipped so badly; and, he whips now worse than he did. They say he is getting crazy, he whips so badly."[40] In Illinois, a local boy's "back, sides, and hips, exhibited incontrovertible proof that he had been placed under the tuition of one who knew how to torture as well as to teach." Another teacher was fired for raising an iron stove poker over the heads of his students.[41] Richard Henry Dana, who would condemn corporal punishment for sailors in *Two Years before the Mast* (1840), as well as for enslaved people in the American South, drew his opinions at least partially from childhood memories. He recalled with horror the use of a "long pine ferule" with which the teacher struck delinquents, and an instance in which a teacher tore off part of his ear while dragging him across the room. After Dana returned from an illness, the same teacher accused him of playing sick and began to whip him. "Upon this hand he inflicted six blows with all his strength," Dana wrote,

> and then six upon the right hand. I was in such a frenzy of indignation at his injustice and his insulting insinuations that I could not have uttered a word for my life. . . . He called for my right hand again and gave six more blows in the same manner and then six more upon the left. My hands were swollen and in acute pain, but I did not flinch or show a sign of suffering. He was determined to conquer and gave six more blows upon each hand, with full force. Still there was not sign from me of pain or submission.

Dana eventually complained to the trustees of the school, and the teacher was fired. The same pitched confrontations, ostensibly over matters of principle, played out between armed men and subordinate children all across the country.[42]

It is difficult to estimate the incidence of punishment in any given classroom. The decentralization of school governance during the nineteenth century made systematic data collection impossible, especially regarding disciplinary practices. The records that do exist pose challenges to verification or generalization. In Ohio, for example, a German schoolmaster claimed to have meticulously recorded the punishments he had administered over fifty-one years of teaching. It is quite a list.

1,115,800	Raps on the head
911,527	Blows with a cane
136,715	Blows with the hand
124,010	Blows with a rod
20,989	Blows with a ruler
12,235	Blows over the mouth
7,905	Boxes on the ear
1,707	Holding up the rod
777	Kneeling on peas
613	Kneeling on a triangular block of wood[43]

If these numbers are accurate, a single teacher administered hundreds of strokes every day that he spent in the classroom, a number that beggars the imagination. Other estimates are more modest, yet they also speak to a flood of punishment in the schools. Horace Mann tallied an average of sixty floggings a day in a Boston school he visited during the mid-nineteenth century. As an opponent of such methods, Mann may have chosen an outlying example, but there is no way to be sure. By the 1880s, the Boston schools were officially reporting 11,678 cases of physical punishment per year, nearly the number of the city's entire student body—yielding a daily average similar to Mann's, although spread across more schools.[44] Whether or not one accepts the philosophical tenets of corporal punishment, the reality was prone to incidents of abuse, and (as we will discuss in chapter 3) these abuses continued long after the end of the nineteenth century, a further reason to doubt the efficacy of physically punishing schoolchildren and to resist any calls for its return.

In many areas of the country, classroom whippings had begun to fade by the late nineteenth century. Just as the disorganization of rural schoolhouses lent itself to corporal punishment, the rise of larger educational systems—championed by Mann and others—came to discourage it. There were several reasons for the correlation. First, the rise of official record keeping "no doubt had the effect of mobilizing public opinion [against corporal punishment] and of keeping it alive to the issue." More importantly, hierarchical systems of authority tended to formalize and routinize teacher behavior. As early as 1846, the New York City schools established uniform procedures to govern corporal punishment. "Mild punishments shall be used in all cases where the same can be made effectual," noted the bylaws. "Corporal punishment shall be resorted to only in special cases, and shall be used with great discretion." Only the principal teacher, not assistants or student monitors, was allowed to whip pupils, and he could not administer the punishment in the presence of other students. After each punishment, the principal had to record the name of the pupil and the offense in a book designated for that purpose.[45] Similar provisions were present in most urban school systems by the end of the century, stating that students could be subjected to corporal punishment only after proving "disorderly or refractory" and with written consent from the principal or the school committee.[46] It is unclear how scrupulously schools adhered to these procedures, and it bears mentioning that urban school reformers merely hoped to regulate corporal punishment rather than abolish it entirely; most accepted the practice as a measure of last resort. Nevertheless, the rise of public school systems in the mid-nineteenth century marked a structural and rhetorical shift away from whipping and the disciplinary authority of individual teachers.[47]

For their part, many teachers welcomed these changes as a means of increasing their professional status. "Much has been said . . . on the subject of *elevating* the profession of the teacher," one wrote, but if teachers were not accorded the respect of ministers, doctors, or lawyers, it was because "there is aroused in the mind of every sensitive, kind-hearted, and benevolent person, a feeling of indignation towards any *man* who strikes a *boy*. Legalize it—throw the sanctions of custom around it—do what you will—still it is, in reality, *unmanly* and *undignified*." Only as teachers ceased to act as bullies would their reputations rise. Anticipating arguments that would reappear in the twentieth century, teachers began to insist that punishment fell outside their area of professional expertise, and worried that striking a child could expose them to legal liability and cost them their jobs.[48]

Besides issues of professionalism, the foremost objections to corporal punishment returned to its effects on students. Opponents worried that whipping inhibited students' self-regulation and warped their emotions, inflaming vengeance and suppressing tenderness. These objections, too, were tied to broad changes in American society and thought, which by the early nineteenth century had led to the disciplinary alternatives of shame and moral suasion.

Liberalism and Shame

A second approach to punishing schoolchildren was to replace physical suffering with psychic suffering, particularly through public humiliation. The associated techniques were neither novel nor entirely distinct from corporal punishment: variations had been used in schools well before the nineteenth century, and many incorporated elements of pain or fatigue. Teachers commonly scolded students in front of classmates, made them sit with children of the opposite sex, or perched them on a stool wearing some symbol of misbehavior or ignorance. Some used dunce caps, though not as early or as widely as popular culture suggests. (The first popular literary reference came from Charles Dickens in the 1840s.)[49] Others kept placards denoting common offenses, such as lying, stealing, or sleeping, that they hung around students' necks. Some forced pupils to cut a small branch from a tree, which the teacher would whittle into the shape of a clothespin and attach to their noses.[50] In at least one memorable case, children were hung from the ceiling in a basket.[51]

What makes shame interesting is less its methods of application than the broader systems of discipline in which it was embedded. While the practice of corporal punishment aligned with premodern, agrarian sensibilities, by the beginning of the nineteenth century opponents contended that whipping had fallen out of step with religious conceptions of free will, with democratic-republican politics, and with an emerging capitalist marketplace. These arguments sprang from a liberal worldview that took the individual, rather than the family or the community, as the foundational unit of society and prioritized personal freedom and self-control as the wellsprings of moral behavior. Physical punishment could perhaps secure a person's obedience to established authorities, ran the new line of thinking, but it could never develop the conscience necessary for civic virtue. Instead, educational reformers experimented with new forms of discipline based on group interactions and self-policing, in which the individual internalized the watchful gaze of others and, eventually, self-governed by their judgments. When applied to punishment, this scrutiny was channeled into feelings of shame.

A few words are in order before we discuss historical justifications and criticisms of the new methods. First, readers should recognize that shame relies on emotion rather than reason, and that many of its applications in schools were purely behavioristic: that is, they conditioned students to avoid misbehavior without recourse to moral choice, an obvious paradox given that liberals hoped to train deliberative citizens and discerning consumers. Readers should also note that shame is normative, holding students to moral standards that are no less restrictive for being diffuse and unspoken. To judge oneself against public norms is to uncritically accept the authority of convention and to deny the possibility of diverse ways of being. This, too, raises an element of paradox insofar as many liberal social theorists denounced the tyranny of public opinion.[52] Finally, while some writers have argued that shame is intrinsic to the human condition and, as a disciplinary regime, best accords with mankind's natural propensities, there was nothing natural about its tightly choreographed deployment in nineteenth-century classrooms. It was a system that required deliberate propagation and went hand in hand with modern changes in religion, politics, and economics.[53]

Just as corporal punishment found sanction in religious rhetoric, so too did the use of shame. During the Great Awakening of the mid-eighteenth century, Methodists, New Light Presbyterians, and other Protestant denominations sought to revitalize churchgoing with an emphasis on public conversions and the role of personal choice and emotion in salvation. Unitarians and Quakers went even further, downplaying the role of human depravity altogether to celebrate the Inner Light and the potential for individual divinity. Meanwhile, from the pulpit, the college, and the schoolhouse, religious leaders propounded the tenets of Scottish commonsense philosophy, arguing that individuals possessed an innate moral faculty that enabled them to perceive God's handiwork and to comport themselves according to His will. In each of these cases, the image of sinful children needing physical correction evolved into one of individual souls facing moral choices. Making the right decisions required God-given reason and emotional sensitivity, the very qualities that whipping threatened to suppress. Increasingly, then, theological liberals—those who prioritized free will—spoke out against whipping schoolchildren and became the first to experiment with alternative forms of punishment.[54]

The rise of colonial self-government and the revolt against the British monarchy also forced reformers to question modes of punishment in the schoolroom. Student discipline was bound up with civic education generally, and on this topic the writings of John Locke became especially important. For Locke, representative self-government both attested to the fact of self-governing individuals—those who could control their passions, overcome self-interest, and comport themselves according to their own sense of reason—and depended on the cultivation of such individuals from childhood. "All virtue and excellency lies in a power of denying ourselves the satisfaction of our own desires," he wrote, "where reason does not authorize them."[55] Locke encouraged parents to instill this sort of rationality by discussing ethical matters with children as soon as possible and cautioned against plying them with sweets or toys.[56] He opposed corporal punishment for the same reasons. Whipping children was coercive, sensual rather than rational, and too often an arbitrary exercise of tyranny. "Such a slavish discipline," he wrote, "makes a slavish temper," unfit for free citizens. It could only break children's spirits, causing them to "lose all their vigor and industry," or encourage duplicity and vengeance within them. Because the source of discipline remained external, "the child submits, and dissembles obedience, whilst the fear of the rod hangs over him; but when that is removed, and, by being out of sight, he can promise himself impunity, he gives the greater scope to his natural inclination." For Locke, physical pain could never call forth the government of reason.[57]

While reason was the focus of Locke's teaching, emotional sensitivity continued to play an important role in his methods. Recognizing that individuals are more susceptible to pain than pleasure and often prefer the arbitrary moral codes with which they are raised, Locke encouraged parents to instill early in children "a love of credit and an apprehension of shame and disgrace," through which they could most effectively align the child's behavior with reason. Indeed, Locke noted that no "correction [could be] useful to a child, where the shame of suffering for having done amiss, does not work more upon him than the pain."[58] Scholars have debated the implications of this approach. It is hardly the case, as some critical readers claim, that Locke intended to manipulate children, leaving "the Lockean (and indeed liberal) subject . . . deeply disciplined and thoroughly normalized, and as a result, governed more by habitual values than rational reflection or autonomous cal-culation."[59] The habits being instilled were precisely those necessary to *resist* regimentation or manipulability, "the goal of early habituation [being] not to program future behavior, but to inculcate physical and mental flexibility," and rather than ensnaring children in a desire for credit and an aversion to shame, Locke's approach moved past those aspects as quickly as possible, fortifying the child's mind with "the discipline, skepticism, and modesty necessary to think clearly in the face of the hostile forces arranged against such thought."[60]

Nevertheless, tracing Locke's influence through subsequent generations of philosophy demonstrates how shame could be decoupled from the exercise of reason, and here the critics find stronger footing. By the late eighteenth century, commonsense philosophy was shifting from Locke's emphasis on natural *reason* to an emphasis on natural *sympathy*, propounded by moral sentimentalists like Francis Hutcheson, who argued that human beings had inborn and emotional feelings about right and wrong, and eventually to the writings of Adam Smith and David Hume, for whom moral sympathy was not simply an innate attribute but a socially cultivated one. In its positive manifestations, sympathy encouraged students to imagine the feelings of oth-ers and presaged many of the Romantic approaches outlined below.[61] On the other hand, focusing on emotional ties heightened students' susceptibility to the approval or reprobation of teachers and peers—in short, to shame. Lines of intellectual influence can be diffuse: shaming practices in the United States long predated Smith and Hume, whose writings responded to latent social changes as much as they drove them. It is enough here to say that the ten-sions around shame and liberalism were present but largely unremarked on through the eighteenth and nineteenth centuries. American commentators repeated Locke's recommendations, criticizing corporal punishment as an impediment to citizenship and offering shame as the appropriate alternative, even as changing educational contexts attenuated Locke's original rationale.[62]

Nevertheless, this intellectual lineage highlights a key issue for educa-tors regarding shame tactics. Civic education seems to require instilling both an appropriate concern for the feelings and standards of the community (as Hume stressed) and an ability to think independently and autonomously (as Locke demanded). Recall the idea that punishment has an expressive func-tion, giving voice to community disapproval, and also that the specific form of a punishment has "secondary expressions": it conveys meanings beyond vague disapproval. Shame tactics imply a deep concern for social opinion— that we should care for the approval of others in what we say and do—but the civic implications of this secondary expression are mixed. With respect to shame-oriented punishments, there seems to be a difficult line to walk between emphasizing a concern for social values—what others think—and helping students think creatively and critically about new possibilities.

Just as new political paradigms challenged the authoritarian nature of the classroom, so did economic modernization. An emergent market economy demanded individualism, competition, risk-taking, and acquisitiveness from its participants. In order to seek their own self-interest, and thereby contribute to the order and prosperity of society as a whole, students needed to cultivate a work ethic, delay gratification, and police their own thoughts and actions. Schools imparted these skills through emulation, pitting students against their peers in explicitly competitive learning environments.[63] Emulative methods predated public education, finding fullest expression in the academies and charity schools of the early nineteenth century, from which public schools arose and with which they initially competed. The two institutions served different populations of students. Academies, much like latter-day high schools, offered instruction in higher branches of learning to adolescents from a variety of social backgrounds, while charity schools provided rudimentary lessons to children of impoverished families. Yet both emerged in commercial settings—either cities or market towns—and responded to different social challenges than the one-room schools of the countryside did. Confronted with the visible effects of unemployment and street crime, in particular, they promoted emulation as a path to individual and social order.

Academies incorporated emulation through competitive exhibitions, both on a daily basis in front of teachers or the school's trustees and in end-of-term performances for the entire town.[64] Teachers bestowed books, prizes, certificates, and medals on the students who spoke the most eloquently, but more than that promised "the unfading Garlands of praise which applauding audiences shall bestow." Indeed, teachers sought to "rouse" students through the use of structured competition and "enkindle the sparks of Ambition to an ardent blaze." Children not only strove for the awards, they also struggled to outpace the "mortifying obscurity" of mediocrity or the outright shame of failure. Critics questioned both the efficacy and ethics of this sort of motivation. Many worried that "jealousy and envy, under the specious semblance of emulation," would poison the classroom atmosphere, while others questioned how status-hungry competitors could continue to respect their less ambitious parents or neighbors.[65] There were also struggles to refine competition in such a way that all students remained engaged. As one observer pointed out, once children discovered "that all of them could not obtain the medal . . . the contention continued sometimes among three, but seldom with more than two."[66] How could competition instill camaraderie rather than resentment or feelings of superiority, and how could it motivate students once it became obvious that they were no longer in the running for a prize?

Possible answers to these questions emerged from charity schools, which took emulation to even greater extremes and assigned it more explicit spatial dimensions. In the first decades of the nineteenth century, Joseph Lancaster, an English Quaker, developed a system of instruction that allowed a single teacher to supervise hundreds of students, an economy of scale with obvious appeal to cash-strapped charity schools in both England and the United States. In Lancaster's schools every movement was planned and lessons were broken into their smallest component parts for memorization and recitation. At a signal from the teacher, the students divided into ability groups, each led by a student monitor, in which they competed to master information printed on large flash cards. Those who failed languished, while those who succeeded were awarded tickets redeemable for books and trinkets and eventually rose to the next class, a visible testament to their abilities and a finer-tuned incentive than emulation alone. Lancaster was a critic of corporal punishment, and his plan purposely limited disciplinary action by the teacher. So coordinated were Lancaster's classrooms that movement could play out with almost no adult intervention at all. The layout of the schools was such that each student was subject to the eyes of his or her monitor, and the whole to the eyes of the teacher. Thus, if competition was the impetus that kept the mechanism moving, it was the psychology of sight lines—of seeing oneself through the eyes of others—that kept it from spinning out of control.[67]

Again, all this was of a piece with early nineteenth-century thinking. As the historian Dell Upton has observed, commonsense philosophy, Newtonian physics, and free-market economics all took as their subjects "the coordinated behavior of apparently independent physical bodies" and the "invisible coordination" of the universe, of which visible order was a complementary reflection. By the same logic, political theorists argued that routinizing children's self-interest through "carefully conceived spatial arrangements" could "direct civic life into appropriate channels," instilling a sense of camaraderie and squaring individual freedom with the public good. Thus, both academies and Lancaster schools mirrored republican conceptions of space and order. They were "transparent, or open to inspection and understanding by all comers; classified, or ordered by uniform categories based on essential similarities among disparate components; and articulated, or characterized by flexible and individually manipulable relationships."[68] Harmonizing individuals through internalized surveillance and public shame extended the reliance on emotional conditioning to a broader type of social control, which the social theorist Michel Foucault would later describe as the "internalized gaze," a form of "capillary power" underlying all modern disciplinary technologies.[69]

Although Foucault did not reference schools specifically, he based his critique on Jeremy Bentham's panopticon—an eighteenth-century proposal for prisons in which inmates were isolated and subjected to constant surveillance—which Bentham, in turn, fully intended to apply to education. Bentham championed the Lancaster system in his writing and corresponded with several charity schools in America. Governing students through shame seemed to maximize the outcomes of education while minimizing the time, cost, and physical pain of learning, and thus fulfilled Bentham's goal of achieving the greatest happiness for the greatest number. Of the children subjected to these unsparing judgments, he wrote, "Call them soldiers, call them monks, call them machines, so they were but happy ones, I should not care."[70] Of course, it was debatable whether children were in fact happy when locked in competitive struggle. As Bentham himself acknowledged, "Never can the matter of reward be obtained, to pour into one bosom, but at the expense of suffering, however, remote and disguised, inflicted upon others."[71] Critics in the United States and in England objected to the mechanistic use of shame in charity schools just as they did to emulation in the academies. Even staunch opponents of whipping wrote that "bodily pain is nothing to the sting of shame, nothing to the burning anguish produced by the sense of insult, inhumanity, and injustice." "As the best boys are always most alive to shame," noted the poet Robert Southey, these methods "[rendered] punishment more severe precisely in proportion to the good qualities of the offender" and inculcated a "resentful and malicious disposition." Samuel Coleridge likewise decried the "soul-benumbing ignominy" of Lancaster schools, which reveled "in repression, and possible after-perversion of the natural feelings."[72]

Although shame was a powerful ideological ideal, like whipping it was never as totalizing as critics feared. As the historian Carl Kaestle observes, the Foucauldian vision of an all-encompassing system of control may be criticized "for overlooking causal factors external to the social system, and for de-emphasizing persistent elements of dysfunction, indifference, and independence within the system."[73] In this case, while Lancaster schools offered "highly aestheticized, titillating glimpses of what republican society *might* be," in practice they alienated both parents and students, who resented their purely rote learning and began to seek other educational opportunities.[74] Lancaster schools had fallen from favor by the 1830s, and common-school reformers strenuously distanced themselves from their worst excesses. There was a growing awareness of the teacher's role in promoting student behavior and misbehavior and of the school's role in co-constructing student actions.

Reliance on pride and shame persisted in individual classrooms—not to mention through publicly posted grades, honor rolls, class rankings, and valedictory speeches—but as a systematic practice, public shame gave way to gentler forms of coercion.[75]

Romanticism and Moral Suasion

If corporal punishment was out of step with the political and economic ideals of the nineteenth century, it was even more misaligned with the era's emotional sensibilities. With a rising middle class came an increasingly private domestic sphere, largely defined by gentle manners and tender visions of childhood. New approaches to teaching and learning, drawn from the writings of Jean-Jacques Rousseau, Johann Pestalozzi, Friedrich Froebel, and a generation of Romantic poets and essayists, emphasized the innocence of children, who needed nurture rather than correction at school, and sought to pattern the classroom on the sheltered environment of the middle-class home. To the extent that they favored any punishment at all, Romantic reformers advocated a policy of "moral suasion," in which kindness and emotional affection elicited good behavior and wrongdoing prompted introspection and remorse.[76] These reactions were predicated on sympathy with one's teachers and classmates, and it is no accident that they coincided with the feminization of teaching or the development of cooperative learning environments like kindergartens. Nor is it surprising that they overlapped with campaigns to improve the treatment of enslaved people, convicts, sailors, and animals. The humanitarian crusades of the mid-nineteenth century depended on expansive sentimentality and a faith in the inherent goodness of children, a stance reflected and contrived by schools themselves.[77]

Romantics condemned corporal punishment for many of the same reasons that Locke had, complaining that it "repressed students from wrongdoing but did not reform their consciences."[78] Attentive as they were to children's emotions, Romantics tended to be even more concerned about inflaming vengeance or desensitizing students to violence, which they referred to as "hardening" the child. As one opponent of corporal punishment wrote, "Whipping in the school-room in the presence of the scholars is the same, in its demoralizing and hardening influence on the pupils who witness it, as the public whipping in the park."[79] John Griscom, a New York school reformer, compared physical punishment to the "'sting of a venomous insect,' which warped a child's moral character by arousing feelings of revenge and anger." William C. Woodbridge, editor of the *American Annals of Education*, argued that whipping "kindled [a child's] evil dispositions and passions," leading to obstinacy and bullying.[80] Conversely, "a child, who has always been kindly treated by his parents and has never been flogged by them, or seen pain inflicted on others, [would] be kind to his brothers and sisters. Such a child [would] also be kind to the domestic animals, the cat, the dog, &c, and will not strike or kick them, or pull them or push them rudely."[81] By treating students gently and relying on the "law of kindness," teachers could secure not merely compliance with classroom rules but also the mutual recognition and respect necessary for compassion and guilt.[82]

There were subtle but important distinctions between Romantic notions of guilt and earlier references to shame. Whereas the latter was a public phenomenon that targeted the student's entire being and depended on internalizing the judgment of others, the former was a private transgression of trust that originated within one's own conscience and tended to focus on the misdeed rather than the person as a whole.[83] As several scholars have observed, shame threatened to overwhelm students with "a deep feeling of inadequacy," while guilt offered the possibility of repentance and growth, in keeping with the schools' broader mission of self-culture and the Romantics' hope of loving reform.[84] Common disciplinary techniques included separation from the group, whether by reseating students in a corner or suspending them altogether; forgoing privileges such as private reading time or recess; and requiring restitution for breaches of etiquette, ranging from personal apologies to the dreaded "I shall not . . ." phrases copied out on the blackboard. As with all punishments, these techniques were most successful when leavened with emotional appeals and reasoned explanations, without which they lost the virtues of both deterrence and reconciliation.

The incorporation of affective discipline originated in the Northeast between the 1820s and the 1850s.[85] Early adherents, including Timothy Dwight, Samuel Read Hall, and Francis Wayland, drew heavily from the writings of the Swiss educator Johann Pestalozzi and contended that "children were governed far more easily by affection, reason, moral principle, and the uniform, fair, and impartial application of school rules than by 'the whip and ferule.'"[86] These authors were also critical of emulative techniques, which, they warned, "cannot fail to strengthen the selfish principles of our nature."[87] Wayland, in particular, worried about the crass materialism of the emerging capitalist society and sought to prioritize moral compassion over selfish competition in the classroom. To "guard, control and direct" children's emotions, to bring them "under the dominion of the understanding," educators could not rely only on the baser instincts. Educating the whole child required teachers to model sympathy and self-control in their own actions, to elicit cooperation by befriending children, and to match praise or punishment to the particular gifts of each child, taking each child's abilities and stage of development into account. Thus, teachers should "render the school pleasant to those who compose it," urged Samuel Read Hall, so that students might come "to think of study as a pleasure, and delight in it." If students disregarded the rules, the most effective consequence would be their own conscience. Teachers would de-emphasize invidious comparisons between students, and no more would they punish students for different levels of achievement, provided that each child fulfilled his or her potential.[88]

The leading voices of the common-school reform movement—among them Horace Mann, Horace Eaton, Henry Barnard, and Catharine Beecher—were also supporters of affective discipline. These writers argued that, just as hierarchical governance and record keeping discouraged the arbitrary exercise of corporal punishment, a professional teaching corps, trained in child study (what we might now call educational psychology), could do away with not only corporal punishment but also the "rules, prizes, demerits, marks, and the entire repressive apparatus which bribed or threatened children into being industrious and orderly," replacing them with engaging lessons, cooperative exercises, and gentle correction. Indeed, controlling the classroom humanely would become the hallmark of the qualified teacher, a testament to her training and her worthiness of public trust.[89]

The gender pronouns in the previous sentence are noteworthy. As outlined earlier in this chapter, corporal punishment relied on a male teacher's strength to subdue older students. Not all male teachers were comfortable exerting this power—one could construct an interesting reading list from the sensitive, thoughtful men who refused to whip their pupils, including Amos Bronson Alcott, Henry David Thoreau, Walt Whitman, and (probably) John Dewey.[90] Nevertheless, the emerging nexus between professionalism and emotional discipline facilitated a shift from male teachers to female teachers during the mid-nineteenth century. It seemed a natural development, given the era's assumptions about women's nurturing dispositions. "What qualified particular women for teaching positions was their character and reputation," notes historian B. Edward McClellan. "Even tough-minded reformers were willing to forgive a woman 'her ignorance of syntax and low level of scholarship' if she had 'common sense and a good heart.'"[91] Proponents insisted that women's "native tact" would necessarily lead "to the improvement of manners and morals in schools, since females attach more importance to them than men; and they have a peculiar power of awakening the sympathies of children, and inspiring them with a desire to excel."[92] Whether their appeal was maternal in the case of younger children or openly (if chastely) erotic for older students, it was widely accepted that women could elicit good behavior without recourse to violence.[93]

Female students were supposed to have a similar civilizing influence on their male classmates, replacing "the rudeness and *abandon* which prevails among boys" with continence and self-restraint.[94] Yet boys could corrupt girls as easily as girls uplifted boys, and that raised difficult questions about classroom punishment. When moral suasion failed, could girls be whipped? For many educators, the notion was unthinkable. One noted that his remarks in favor of corporal punishment were "directed entirely to the management of *boys*, believing, as I do, that no female pupil or child (*unless abandoned beyond any hope*), will ever require physical force to cause her to submit to wholesome rules and regulations." "I will not so degrade myself," he continued, "as to make use of the word *girl* or *female* . . . in connexion with the subject of *flogging*."[95] Others worried that, "in a mixed school, [if] a boy and a girl were to commit the same offense, a teacher might be accused of partiality if he did not punish them in the same way," but "if he makes the flesh of the girl tremble under the rod or the ferule, he is liable to be charged with undue severity." Some schoolmasters insisted on erecting a partition between the male and female sides of the classroom for just this reason, so that different disciplinary standards could reign in each.[96] All of these comments played on essentialist notions of femininity, of course, and should not be taken at face value. Girls did misbehave and were whipped as well as boys, if not as frequently.[97] A famous scene in Louisa May Alcott's *Little Women* (1868) features Amy, the youngest sister, caught with contraband limes in her desk, for which the teacher repeatedly smacks her palm with a ruler and makes her stand in front of the class in shame.[98]

While female teachers facilitated the move away from corporal punishment overall, they did not always receive the training and support to avoid it and did not shy from using it when circumstances seemed to dictate its application. A teacher in North Dakota whose students had reduced her to tears over the winter term had regained control by July. "I had the pleasure of giving a little chap a whipping," she wrote in her journal, and, on another occasion, "I had to keep two scholars [after school] this evening, and that is not all I did for them, the little rascals."[99] In Massachusetts, one woman punished her female students by tying their thumbs to her chair, and another dangled little boys out the window. As an older student observed, "After ten or twenty years of strenuous teaching, a woman can become as hard-boiled as any man; in fact, some of them are that way when they begin. The worst cut I ever received from a switch in my boyhood, I took on the back of my bare calves from a woman teacher."[100]

The ideals of moral suasion were compelling for many teachers and had significantly shifted the norms of student punishment by the end of the nineteenth century. As with earlier forms of discipline, however, they fell short of universal adoption. As long as educators confronted long hours in over-crowded classrooms, "[even] the wisest [were] tempted to adopt violent means, to proclaim martial law, corporal punishment, mechanical arrange-ments, bribes, spies, wrath, main strength and ignorance, in place of that wise and genial providential influence they had hoped ... to adopt."[101] Moral appeals became a preventative strategy for classroom management but were only the first option in an escalating series of punishments rather than an end unto themselves. Few parents, teachers, or administrators found them suffi-cient in cases of serious disobedience. Thus, schools became relatively gentler places for children, but for functional reasons rather than as a result of any new philosophical consensus.

Conclusion

A fitting close to our discussion of school punishment in early America comes from a description of Anthony Benezet, a White Quaker educator and aboli-tionist who, in the late eighteenth century, founded schools for Black children. In many ways, Benezet was profoundly out of step with his contemporaries. During an era when most Americans were pessimistic about Black citizen-ship and many actively suppressed educational opportunities for non-White children—going so far as to burn and ransack schools—Benezet taught not merely as an act of charity or racial uplift but also as a demonstration of his students' innate intellectual and moral equality and thus as an argument for their civil rights. Benezet was also unusual in how he corrected his students, albeit in ways more closely related to his context. Benezet's method, notes an early biographer, "[was] that of mildness. He investigated the natural dispo-sitions of his pupils, and adapted his management of them, to their various tempers. Persuasion would secure attention and obedience in some, while proper excitement to emulation, would animate and encourage others. The sense of shame, and the fear of disgrace, could be roused in the minds of those, whose stubbornness the less acute remedies would not affect; so that he rarely had recourse to corporal punishment, and seldom permitted an angry passion to be exhibited to his scholars."[102] This account captures the entire cycle of nineteenth-century school punishments, from corporal punishment to shame to moral suasion, in the work of a single educator at the very outset of the era. Although the description was meant to be complimentary, Bene-zet's multifaceted approach also speaks to the failure of any single ideology to solve the problem of student misbehavior. To suggest that different pun-ishments are apt for different students at different times may say little at all, and the fact that all options remained on the table, even for a well-meaning Quaker, suggests that moral progress in school discipline would come with significant provisos.

Other experimental educators met with similar frustrations. In establishing a utopian colony in New Lanark, Scotland, for example, the industrialist Robert Owen instituted a behaviorist approach that mobilized public shame in ways reminiscent of the Lancaster system. Its crowning achievement was the "silent monitor," a forebear of today's behavior charts, in which a colored block next to a worker represented the quality of that person's deportment. Black represented bad conduct, blue and yellow were middling, and white was exemplary. It is unclear whether the method continued at Owen's second colony, in New Harmony, Indiana, which emphasized Pestalozzi's methods of emotional reform, but for Owen the approaches sprang from the same impulse—namely, "immediate social disapproval of [the child's] offensive activities," combined with a rational explanation of "why [his behavior] was wrong, why it might cause someone unhappiness, and why, therefore, it would lead ultimately to his own unhappiness."[103] Amos Bronson Alcott, an admirer and imitator of Owen, combined a belief in the innate goodness of children with similarly questionable methods of discipline. Rather than imposing adult authority in the classroom, Alcott encouraged students to inform on one another, telling them to "write in their journals the name of any student they felt had done something not in accordance with 'moral rectitude.'" "Each Saturday," notes his biographer, "these names were read, the persons accused were tried and, if found guilty, had to make a public apology. This, Alcott thought, would make 'improper conduct' unpopular and render corporal punishment unnecessary." Predictably, both Owen's and Alcott's utopian experiments failed before their methods could redeem humanity as a whole.[104]

How should one interpret these halting, evolving, and overlapping approaches to punishment? It may be tempting to see Benezet, Owen, and Alcott as harbingers of a gradually unfolding progress, in which educators steadily matured from brutality to gentleness or from physical correction to spiritual correction. Many contemporaries took exactly that perspective, drawing on Hegelian philosophy to argue that "inflicting bodily pain is the lowest form of superiority" and that "every new accession of spiritual power supersedes the necessity of appealing to the brute part of human nature." As civilization advanced, they thought, harsh punishments would steadily fade away.[105] This change was especially important for students who, according to the era's racist explanations of cultural difference, were transitioning from "primitive" cultures to a higher state of "civilization" for the first time, particularly those students from formerly enslaved and newly colonized populations. For example, in the decade after the Civil War, the organizers of freedmen's schools in the South were adamant that teachers use affection and reason rather than corporal punishment with Black pupils. While it could be challenging to manage students "just emerging into the blessings of self-control," they argued that an effective teacher could secure order "without any severity of treatment, but by the persuasions which flow from the teacher's own character and example." "Whipping may do for slaves," noted General O. O. Howard, the director of the Bureau of Refugees, Freedmen, and Abandoned Lands, "but freedmen should do right without it."[106]

These prescriptions offered an inspiring ideal, but by accepting prevailing hierarchies of civilization and punishment, they did not fundamentally challenge the supposed inferiority of non-White children. Drawing from the same tenets, some White teachers simply decided to beat civilization into their students.[107] The disparity between official policy and classroom practice was probably starkest in the boarding schools created to assimilate Native Americans, where students were entirely separated from their communities and subject to military regulations. Here, too, official policy recommended the use of "'moral measures' and light punishments" for infractions, but school leaders were less optimistic about their success. Thomas J. Morgan, the commissioner of Indian Affairs during the 1890s, complained that boarding schools were full of children who "are naturally brutish and whose training has developed their anima and left their higher nature underdeveloped." Such impulsivity could not be curbed through moral means, he claimed, but required "corporal punishment, confinement, deprivation of privileges, or restriction of diet." Beatings at boarding schools were common through the early twentieth century, as were forced labor and prolonged isolation in cells or closets.[108]

Emerging paradigms of evolutionary biology also weakened notions of intellectual and moral progress. Drawing from Darwinist theories of ontogenic recapitulation—the idea that each organism's growth retraces the development of the entire species—some educators pointed out that "although the progress of the race [as a whole] is away from the brute, the individual who is born into the world is, biologically, no farther away from the brute than was the infant who was born at the very dawn of human progress." Because children were developmentally oriented toward physical sensation, these writers argued, the steady abolition of corporal punishment in the adult world did not necessarily disqualify its use on children.[109] Such pseudoscientific theories may explain the historical puzzle of why whipping and the use of shame lasted far longer within schools than they did outside of them, and (again) why physical punishments fell on immigrants and children of color longer and more frequently than they did on native-born White children.

We reject narratives of spiritual progress or biological determinism in school punishment, although both interpretations linger into the present. First, we see little evidence of moral progress through the nineteenth century. Disciplinary methods went through multiple permutations, but these had less to do with the inherent rightness of any approach than with the cultural de-mands of particular times and places. Uneven patterns of development, com-bined with the institutional conservatism of schools, ensured that responses to the issue remained as varied and confused at the end of the nineteenth century as they were at the beginning. Successive waves of disciplinary re-form layered on top of one another, leaving a palimpsest of punishment—ad hoc, incoherent, and inequitably applied. Readers should therefore resist vi-sions of progress or a false sense of superiority, as the core problems of school punishment remain unresolved today.[110]

Nor do we accept that the persistence of older methods of punishment is a testament to their practical or philosophical necessity—that is, the false equivalence of longevity with legitimacy. Corporal punishment was the dom-inant means of correction throughout the nineteenth century. Defenders of the practice often argued that examples of abuse were exaggerated and that previous generations of students seemed to have turned out well enough. We find neither of these to be compelling justifications. Educators at the time also contended that some students or misdeeds were incorrigible with any-thing but corporal punishment. As one exasperated commentator observed, "Where violence is held up as the last resort, it is regarded as a remedy of su-perior efficacy; and, as its operation is usually more speedy than that of moral means, the teacher is tempted to use it not only with stronger faith, but with greater frequency." However, he worried that if corporal punishment were banished, "the teacher would find himself thrown upon his own resources to devise the most appropriate means of government," putting an equally capri-cious, less effective, and no less coercive regime in its place. It seemed like there was no way out.[111]

Reliance on shame and surveillance presented a similar dilemma. Not only could shame inflict traumatic pain on a student's psyche, it usually did so indiscriminately and out of proportion with the student's actions, inflaming the very emotions that reasoned maturity would have the student suppress. Worse, shame shifted the source of punishment—from the teacher to one's peers and, eventually, to oneself—in ways that made it difficult to challenge its basis. As the historian Ronald Butchart points out, "Behaviorist and bureaucratic disciplinary regimes [such as the Lancaster system] legitimate a morality of omniscient authority that generates resistance among the inmates of schools," yet at the same time they "blunt the possibility of students practicing socially acceptable or politically responsible challenges to illegitimate authority." The result may have seemed like the well-ordered freedom that liberal political theorists demanded, but in fact it denied students moral autonomy, offering "few acceptable lessons in justice, community, or compassion."[112] In such cases, the means of ordering individual students—and, through them, the classroom—were irreconcilable with the substantive democratic habits that order was meant to reflect.

To many, moral suasion seemed the most humane means of correction, and we will return to many of its basic assumptions in our own recommendations. Nevertheless, it remained dogged by questions of rigor and efficacy. Critics asked why tenderness should come before sterner notions of duty or excellence, and even proponents wondered if emotional overtures could check all students' misbehavior. By the end of the century, no less an authority than G. Stanley Hall, the famous educational psychologist, grumbled about the loss of coercive methods from years gone by. "The now too common habit of coquetting for the child's favor, and tickling [his] ego with praises and prizes, and pedagogic pettifogging for [his] good will . . . of delaying a whole schoolroom to apply a subtle psychology of motive," Hall wrote, reflected a "sentimental fear of a judicious slap to rouse a spoiled child."[113] The philosopher William James had similar concerns about the turn away from emulation. "Ought we seriously to hope that marks, distinctions, prizes, and other goals of effort, based on the pursuit of recognized superiority, should be forever banished from our schools?" he asked. "As a psychologist, obliged to notice the deep and pervasive character of the emulous passion, I must confess my doubts."[114] If a certain class of reformers subscribed to notions of childhood innocence, the public at large sided with Hall and James. Americans remained dubious of purely affective forms of punishment and were rarely willing to subsidize the professional training or cooperative classroom arrangements necessary for their flourishing. Most approved of a well-placed slap or spanking from time to time. Teachers, for their part, were put in difficult situations, with little education and even fewer resources. They drew on whatever tools they could to maintain control of their classrooms.

These issues were less settled than subordinated during the twentieth century, not by progress or reasoned debate but by new ways of organizing and speaking about schools and students. The context changed much faster than the principles at stake, opening the door to new forms of euphemism and delaying the vital work of public deliberation. Refusal to abolish contradictory modes of punishment not only denied consideration of their suitability but also clouded profound injustices in their implementation, a moral abdication that demands a reckoning. Our purpose in this chapter and the next is to provide the context necessary for that undertaking.

Punishment, Bureaucracy, and Demoralization

At the beginning of Harper Lee's *To Kill a Mockingbird* (1960), Scout Finch, the protagonist, begins first grade in a segregated White school in southern Alabama during the 1930s. Her teacher, Miss Caroline, is fresh out of training. She establishes a crisp but tender rapport with her students, showing them flash cards and reading simple stories and saying, "Oh, my, wasn't that nice?" Scout is confused by the inanity of these lessons, but she does not grasp the dramatic change that they represent. Seated in a fully furnished classroom with children roughly her own age, listening to a professionally trained woman deliver a uniform curriculum and gentle correction to her students? In the rural South these phenomena would have been uncommon for White students a generation earlier and would remain elusive for Black students for a generation hence. Their presence speaks to the gradual success of campaigns to improve public education nationwide.[1] Unfortunately, obstacles to progress remained, personified in the novel by Burris Ewell, the son of White sharecroppers. When Miss Caroline gives Burris advice on delousing his hair, he gets up to leave, saying that he has "done [his] time for this year." "Been comin' to the first day o' the first grade fer three year now," he brags. "Reckon if I'm smart this year they'll promote me to second." Here the reader recognizes another change afoot in American education: the creation of troublesome overaged students as truancy laws pushed impoverished and working-class children out of the workforce and into the school. Administrators complied with the letter of these laws, but Burris's lax attendance and forthcoming promotion suggest that they also hoped to ease noncompliant students through the system as quickly as possible. Horrified at the neglect that Burris has received thus far, Miss Caroline tells him to sit back down. As she does, his face darkens. "You try and make me, missus," he growls. "Ain't

no snot-nosed slut of a schoolteacher ever born c'n make me do nothing!"
And with that, he walks out the door.[2]

Such scenes capture the competing dynamics that emerged from the nineteenth century. As we argued in the last chapter, a professional teaching force
and the increased systemization of schooling were strong inducements away
from whipping and toward more humane forms of punishment. Nevertheless, the prospect of incorrigible students cast doubt on the efficacy of the
new methods. This impasse came into sharper focus during the twentieth
century. School systems expanded and by many metrics improved. With
better-trained teachers, new facilities, and principles of scientific management, they extended education to far greater numbers of children. Still unresolved, however, were the ways that schools would accommodate historically
underserved groups—whether impoverished White students, like Burris, or
students of color, whose presence in the system was increasing as a result of
immigration and desegregation—and how they would cope with rising disciplinary expectations. Voters continued to demand order, affordability, and
academic proficiency, but without the sort of exclusion or authoritarianism
that educators had traditionally used to achieve them. Unable to expel him
and hesitant to whip him, what were teachers to do with Burris Ewell?

Rather than challenging the notion of incorrigibility itself, with its attendant debates about human nature and social organization, school systems fell
back on bureaucratic solutions, using euphemistic misdirection and assur-
ances of professional expertise to deflect scrutiny of punishment practices.
Returning to a distinction that we made in chapter 1, one could say that the
twentieth century witnessed a general shift from *punishment* to *discipline* in
schools. Whereas nineteenth-century educators invoked moral truths even
when morals were not really at stake—for instance, viewing the act of a
child leaving his seat as a transgression of divinely sanctioned authority—
twentieth-century educators veered in the other direction, addressing actions
solely in terms of their efficiency or outcomes rather than their intrinsic morality. A new, therapeutic language emerged, in which misbehavior became
a disruptive force to be managed rather than a moral failing to be punished.
Schools became increasingly reliant on forms of spatial segregation, including ability grouping, special rooms, and the use of detentions and suspensions to deal with unruly students. Whereas teachers were once responsible
for almost all aspects of student comportment and were directly answerable
to parents and the school board, by the early twentieth century a variety of
new entities had emerged to deal with misbehavior—from hall monitors and
guidance counselors to principals and juvenile courts—specializing disciplinary roles within the system but weakening accountability to those outside it.

New approaches facilitated the growth of larger institutions and preserved traditional notions of order and obedience, but, as we will discuss in chapter 4, they failed to uphold many of the central purposes of schooling. For the moment, it is enough to point out that suspensions, while perhaps less traumatic than whipping or public shaming, brought students no closer to an understanding of their wrongdoing or to a sense of reciprocity with classmates. Institutional logic often rendered schools insensitive to children's intellectual and moral development, prioritizing "zero tolerance" policies and subjecting minors to arrest and court involvement, consequences more appropriate to adults. By shielding schools from public criticism, professionalization perpetuated arbitrary and inequitable punishments under the guise of neutrality. Regulation curbed but did not eliminate physical abuse. The persistence of corporal punishment in some areas—and the appearance of armed police officers in others—ensured that threats of force remained palpable to students. Child psychology and classroom management provided a series of labels that helped some children but hurt others. Suspensions, expulsions, and all other forms of discipline increasingly broke along lines of race and class, but attempts to counteract these developments by strengthening children's legal rights (themselves a type of formalist or bureaucratic remedy) achieved limited results. In hindsight, the professionalization of schools seems less about expertise or efficiency than about safeguarding teachers' status, satisfying demands for order, and upholding implicit commitments to White supremacy, all over and against the safety and educational opportunities of individual children.

We want to stress that these arrangements were not inevitable and that meaningful change remains possible. Although we frame school discipline in the twentieth and twenty-first centuries as a product of "professionalization," we recognize that better versions of professionalism are possible. Many of our own recommendations depend on teachers who are well-trained and have room to exercise discretion, and we welcome professional practices that encompass moral considerations, measured judgment, and public accountability. Rather than trusting professionals alone to alter a system designed to safeguard their interests, however, we call for a public reckoning, with its dual sense of just accounting and reasoned consideration. That reckoning will need to play out in schools, communities, legislatures, and courts if we hope to have an equitable and humane approach to punishment in the years to come.[3]

Mental Hygiene and Therapeutic Culture

The predominant change in school punishment over the past century has been the emergence of therapeutic language and remedies in the classroom.

The term "therapy" can obscure as well as reveal elements of the educational past, so we should clarify at the outset that we use the word suggestively rather than literally. Most schools did not actually put students on the psychiatrist's couch or subject wrongdoers to courses of medical treatment, and the decentralization of districts, schools, and individual classrooms makes it difficult to say to what degree particular teachers adopted therapeutic methods.[4] Nevertheless, there was an indisputable turn toward professional and quasi-medical understandings of school discipline by the early 1900s. As psychological study seeped into colleges of education, a new cohort of teachers sought to identify the developmental or environmental causes of student misbehavior and to overcome them through individually tailored, psychologically sound, and minimally coercive means.[5] Beginning with "child study" and "mental hygiene" in the Progressive Era and cresting with psychoanalysis at midcentury, therapeutic methods sought to avoid punishment through improved instruction, accommodation of children's movements and interests, reorganization of the curriculum, and other preventative measures. As one article put it, "There is no such thing as truancy, retardation, and laziness, as those terms are commonly understood. Those things are nothing but symptoms of some deep-lying troubles which need expert treatment."[6] That position may have been an improvement over whipping children, but it is important to recognize that it too could be coercive and discriminatory and that it deflected questions about the basis of professional judgment.

Educators patterned themselves after social scientists by presenting their methods of correction as objective and morally neutral. As Ronald Butchart eloquently states, the therapeutic worldview "placed all authority in the hands of . . . experts whose task was to measure, calibrate and adjust individuals and settings. Stress-free, conflict-free, frictionless lives, orchestrated by benign managers, required no personal authority whatsoever, it seems, whether internalized unconsciously or constructed and embraced consciously."[7] Yet critics complained that this arrangement advanced no higher goal than "adjustment" and, worse, that it remained agnostic about the very norms to which it demanded adherence. For many conservatives, therapeutic approaches abandoned the cultivation of individual character and, by replacing higher truths with arbitrary social mores, left children vulnerable to the insidious influence of peers, media, or the government. In their view, gentle correction constituted a form of soft totalitarianism, in which teachers conditioned the nation's children with little scrutiny of their methods.[8] Writers on the left raised similar objections, noting that therapeutic discipline abrogated the potential radicalism of progressive education, in which schools and children both engaged in reflexive reform, and in its place encouraged conformity and accommodation to a capitalist status quo. To suppress internal or interpersonal conflict, they contended, was to deny the possibility of social change.[9]

Therapeutic discipline was also problematic because of its imprecision and promiscuity. Just as intelligence testing began as one of several diagnostic tools for individuals with developmental delays, only to be wrenched out of context, applied to the entire population, and reduced to a single, determinative measurement, psychological assessments and the disciplinary apparatus that went with them migrated from clinical studies of "delinquents," young children, and adults with mental or emotional pathologies to the student body at large. Untrained educators drew from a variety of therapeutic approaches and employed their tenets selectively and superficially, abandoning the specificity of diagnostic terms for a sort of pop psychology driven by the mandates of classroom order.[10]

Two distinct strands of therapeutic thought emerged between the 1900s and the 1960s. First was a focus on children's internal emotional dynamics that, drawing from Romantic reforms of the nineteenth century, interpreted misbehavior not as evidence of children's depravity but as a form of misdirected energy. Adapting the classroom to the "natural" or "primitive" instincts of the child was central to the writings of G. Stanley Hall, John Dewey, and others and became a cornerstone of the progressive education movement. If educators simply harnessed children's intrinsic motivation, the argument ran, self-regulation would inevitably result, forgoing the need for any sort of punishment. By the 1940s, the work of A. H. Maslow seemed to support this approach, positing a "hierarchy of needs" to which effective teachers would attend.[11] Teaching manuals of the era reflected these ideas, stressing activity and emotional security as "basic needs" of students and the foundation for a functional classroom. To the extent that they discussed punishment at all, it was usually in the context of another instinctual need, sociability, and involved brief exclusion from the group.[12] All of this fell under the rubric of "mental hygiene," a term connotative of health or, for critics, of intellectual sterility. Mental hygienists sought to identify "stress, anxiety, and frustration, and [to find] ways of removing them from a child's life. The child was to be neither [visibly] disciplined nor given a measure of control over her life; she was simply to be understood and her environment engineered and adjusted." Discipline remained operative, of course, but it appeared calmly and with a smile. As the author Erich Fromm wrote, schools began to pretend that "there is *no* authority, that all is done with the consent of the individual. While the teacher of the past said to Johnny, 'You must do this. If you don't, I'll punish you'; today's teacher says, 'I'm sure you'll *like* to do this.' Here, the sanction for disobedience is not corporal punishment, but the suffering face of the [teacher], or what is worse, conveying the feeling of not being 'adjusted,' of not acting as the crowd acts. Overt authority used physical force; anonymous authority employs psychic manipulation."[13]

Unfortunately, while teachers could be trained to channel children's natural impulses, school was only one outlet for instinctual energy and rarely its source. Sigmund Freud's work on neurosis suggested that student misbehavior ultimately derived from sexual or scatological taboos perpetuated within the family. Thus, if a student was aggressive, manipulative, detached, or overly or insufficiently interested in the opposite sex, teachers could ascribe the problem to Oedipus complexes, oral fixations, or any number of other Freudian diagnoses. These judgments had the advantage of being nonspecific and unfalsifiable; they also positioned the school as a remedy to an inherently dysfunctional home environment.[14] It was in that context that teaching manuals from the 1950s called attention to the "anti-social child, the individualist who does not respond to class techniques, the nonconformist, the trouble-maker." Not only did they group these attributes together—equating nonconformity with troublemaking—but, drawing from Freud, they also ascribed these qualities to the influence of an "exceedingly irate . . . incompetent, shrewish mother" or a "sadistic father."[15]

Personality tests, administered to create psychological profiles and improve classroom efficiency, also relied on a sort of secondhand Freudianism. Across the country, elementary school students answered questions like the following:

> Do you have fewer friends than other children?
> Should you mind your folks even when they are wrong?
> Do you wish you could live in some other home?
> Do you feel that no one at home loves you?

Students were also asked whether the following statements applied to them:

> I enjoy soaking in the bathtub.
> Sometimes I tell dirty jokes when I would rather not.
> Dad always seems too busy to pal around with me.[16]

The historian Sarah Igo notes that these diagnostic tools, indiscriminately applied, marked a profound violation of family privacy; they were not only "assessing, analyzing, and guiding the character of the child" in ways traditionally reserved for parents, but also implicitly scrutinizing the behavior of parents themselves.[17] Freud could be put to better uses. The countercultural

Left repeatedly invoked his theories to oppose authoritarian teaching and do away with harsh punishments.[18] But few schools went that far. It was more common for educational authorities to apply Freudian labels to existing categories of students or patterns of misbehavior, and to reinforce the school's prerogative to address them.

A second strand of therapeutic methods relied on behaviorist psychology, which characterized child development not as the unfolding of latent impulses that a teacher could merely accommodate or repress but instead as a response to entirely external forces. By the end of the nineteenth century, many educators were propounding Herbert Spencer's "pleasure-pain hypothesis," the idea that "whenever an instinctive movement results in pain, it tends thereafter to be repressed; whenever it results in pleasure, it tends thereafter to be repeated."[19] For Spencer, human personality was a product of evolutionary imperatives, a means of self-preservation based on discrete experiences. The upshot was that educators could entirely determine children's conduct—indeed, their very identities—through orderly exposure to positive and negative feedback. This kind of environmental conditioning achieved its apex in the mid-twentieth century with the work of B. F. Skinner, an experimental psychologist who pioneered its applications in mental health. Skinner foresaw behaviorism as not merely a clinical treatment but also a form of social planning; he published multiple books on the subject, including a utopian novel that envisioned behavioral modification on a mass scale.[20] The scientific optimism that buoyed these ideas did not survive the 1960s. Between Cold War fears of brainwashing, scientists' complicity in the Vietnam War, and well-publicized cases of ethical malpractice—from the Tuskegee syphilis studies to the Stanford prison experiment—conditioning lost public credibility as a means of social reform. Nevertheless, it persisted in the schools.[21]

As with Freudianism, behaviorism lost most of its nuance in the hands of educators. Classroom iterations remained blunt and overwhelmingly mechanical, focused on compliance with basic procedures rather than self-mastery, confidence building, or other ameliorative goals.[22] Much like in the Lancaster system of the nineteenth century, teachers broke the school day into discrete learning segments and relied on verbal cues and repetition to condition student behavior. One teaching manual offered the following exemplary scene, in which a teacher addresses her pupils: "I said, 'Pencils, down'! John and Rafael and Susan did not respond. We'll try it just with them. John, Rafael, Susan, ready! Pencils, down! Good, John and Rafael. Susan, you were not ready. We'll try it just with you. Susan, only. Pencil down! Good! Now, we'll try it again—all of us. John, Rafael, Susan, ready! Pencils, take! Pencils, down!"[23] Not all behaviorist methods were so mind-numbing. Some could even be fun. Teachers regularly used call-and-response or rhythmic clapping to refocus students, extrinsic rewards such as stars and prizes to motivate them, and demerits or detentions to curb their behavior. However, insofar as these techniques leveraged stimulus-response behaviors and did not engage students in critical reflection or moral transformation, one could raise legitimate concerns about their conceptions of authority and mutual respect, even if most schools lacked the totalitarian environments necessary to condition student behavior fully.[24]

During the 1970s, as school discipline came to dominate national head-lines, instinctual and behavioral approaches combined in a series of com-mercially branded disciplinary strategies.[25] These products differed from one another more in their marketing than in their substance, and few advanced especially novel ideas. At one end of the spectrum, Lee Canter promoted "as-sertive discipline" as a corrective to the purportedly permissive culture of progressive education, with a return to teacher authority and classroom order. Drawing from behaviorist models, Canter stressed the role of immediate pos-itive and negative feedback, modeling, overt directions, and a no-nonsense demeanor.[26] Meanwhile, the psychiatrist William Glasser offered "reality therapy," a developmental approach that rejected passive or nonjudgmental postures to emphasize each child's responsibility to others. Teachers would focus on the consequences of students' actions, setting boundaries and help-ing children meet them.[27] Glasser later shifted to "control theory," which inte-grated basic psychological needs like self-esteem and belonging with choice, responsibility, and compromise. Borrowing from Skinner, he observed that students experimented with different behaviors to achieve their desires. Un-like Skinner, however, he located motivation firmly within the individual and the satisfaction of basic needs, whether those needs were instinctive or in-tegral to one's dignity or self-conception. The latter approach was amenable to constructivist educators, who wanted children to not merely comply with classroom rules but also consent to them. Like many of its predecessors, con-trol theory promised an efficient, nonpunitive path to classroom order.[28]

We do not mean to dismiss the validity of therapeutic approaches in all situations or to imply that their profusion was the result of bad faith. Depend-ing on one's perspective, some of these methods were more effective than others, and all marked a step forward from punishments rooted in vengeance or physical pain. Yet the mere fact that teachers could keep order without whipping did not make these techniques morally acceptable. By privileging professional knowledge and downplaying individual autonomy, the thera-peutic approach often obscured invasions of privacy, contests for power, and debates over moral ends in the classroom. More troubling is that, from their inception, therapeutic techniques underwrote structural regimes that actually worked against students' well-being, reducing therapeutic discipline to a cruel euphemism, almost a contradiction in terms.

Systematizing School Punishment

Therapeutic language caught on because it accorded well with educators' claims to professionalism and to the growing systematization of public education as a whole. As schools grew more complex, specialization and attendant status claims came to dominate the literature of administration and teaching, with dozens of book titles referencing the new science of "classroom management."[29] This language drew from a broader shift toward rules-based bureaucracy in public institutions, a paradigm of expertise that impugned earlier political structures as unenlightened, inefficient, and corrupt. Public participation could actually imperil democracy, reformers warned, by wasting tax money or needlessly duplicating services. With reformers' prompting, older notions of governance—both of students within the classroom and of school districts writ large—gave way to a new faith in social engineering.[30]

The most pervasive disciplinary changes took place in curricular and organizational restructuring rather than in the practice of punishment itself. During the 1920s, child labor laws pushed unprecedented numbers of impoverished and working-class students into the public schools, a cohort that some educators considered a "great army of incapables" with little motivation or intellectual promise.[31] Worried that taxpayers would revolt at the cost of remediating these students and that teachers and parents would resist over-age children in elementary school classrooms, school leaders proposed organizational solutions. First, they lowered standards for advancement, instituting "social promotion" from one grade to the next on the basis of age rather than ability.[32] They also developed forms of in-school segregation to isolate students in dead-end curricular tracks. These placements warehoused underachieving children until they could join the labor force, and in the meantime exempted them from the school's overall promotion rate. Such reforms denied students substantive learning opportunities and undermined the very meaning of educational credentials, since unprepared and sometimes illiterate students could remain in the system through high school. Worse was that administrators framed these changes in strategic but cynically therapeutic terms, promising that children would receive extra support in "'Child Guidance Clinic,' 'Special Class Clinic,' 'Special Education,' 'Psycho-Educational Clinic,' . . . 'Prevocational Education,' [or] 'Adjustment Classes,'" when in fact those students received little more than substandard lessons in hygiene, manual labor, or leisure activities.[33] Curricular tracking offered a repository for not only slow learners but troublemakers as well, whom teachers pushed out of the classroom regardless of their testing results or learning needs. The historian Joseph Tropea documents several ways in which teachers relied on professional discretion to preserve order and subjectively marginalize students. As one contemporary pointed out, while testing was "the guiding principle, still it is by no means closely adhered to, as the condition of the child frequently shows that he should be placed in a special room, even though his classification indicates otherwise."[34] Despite progressive rhetoric about students' academic or emotional profiles, tracking ultimately met teachers' needs, providing a release valve for misbehaving children.

The informal norms behind academic tracks correlated with new, standardized systems of punishment. As school districts grew, they adopted uniform codes of student conduct and sequential disciplinary responses, attempting to eliminate favoritism or abuse by individual teachers. Teachers retained a great deal of discretion under these policies, of course, but by submitting to standard procedures—for instance, issuing written warnings before suspending a student—they could absolve themselves of personal liability and strengthen their professional status. Here readers should note the divergence of two alternative paths: Teachers could have staked professionalism on a broad knowledge of child development, framing punishment as an inextricable aspect of learning and standards of classroom behavior as each teacher's prerogative. Instead, they narrowed their claims to expertise, accepted exogenous disciplinary standards, and abdicated their responsibility to teach children through punishment. Thus, notes the historian Judith Kafka, by attributing misbehavior to "social or emotional maladjustment," teachers could claim that "youth needed therapeutic services beyond the *educational* expertise of a regular classroom teacher," and that punishment was "a specialized task" best suited to "non-instructional personnel," especially school administrators.[35]

For most students, it was only in the early decades of the twentieth century that going to the principal's office became a viable threat. The principalship had theretofore been an ill-defined role, divided between teaching, building supervision, and other duties. As professionalization drew the principal away from the classroom and toward "an administrative culture of authority and discipline," referring students who committed serious infractions to the main office became an efficient way to get troublemakers out of the classroom, freeing teachers to teach.[36] By the 1950s, other disciplinarians appeared in school offices as well, particularly psychological professionals such as guidance counselors and social workers. These were also ill-defined positions. Counselors sometimes ministered to students' emotional needs, sometimes matched a student's academic aptitude with appropriate curricular choices, and sometimes orchestrated a student's suspension. The fact that districts assigned them different titles and different responsibilities makes it difficult to pinpoint their role, but the entire profession of school counseling was organized around soft discipline: the integration of diverse students into a rules-based organization through testing, placement, and environmental adjustment.[37] Large districts undertook a further division of labor when, during the 1970s, they created positions to oversee school security. Soon, security directors had their own journals and conferences, through which they lobbied for stronger disciplinary measures in schools.[38]

With administrative standardization came new reporting requirements. School offices were crowded with filing cabinets full of student dossiers. References to a student's "permanent record" became something of a joke by the 1980s, but it is worth remembering just how permanent these records were for much of the twentieth century.[39] Files documented not only formal disciplinary actions but also personality assessments from teachers, including impressionistic judgments about a student's sexual orientation or predisposition to criminality. This information remained on file throughout a student's academic career. It was often hidden from parents, who had no formal means of appeal, but could be readily reviewed by prospective employers, government agencies, juvenile courts, and the police. Thus, critics observed, "a hastily concluded judgment by an annoyed, impatient third grade teacher could become a lifelong albatross around the neck of an innocent individual," with no means of redress. Only with the Family Educational Rights and Privacy Act (1974) did students gain a statutory right to access their disciplinary records.[40]

Record sharing became the basis for extensive collaboration between government agencies in the correction and control of wayward children. Interlocking welfare services formed a dragnet that some kids could not escape. For example, juvenile courts emerged during the early 1900s as a means to rehabilitate children suspected of wrongdoing. By according judges a great deal of latitude, these courts promised flexible, holistic responses to youthful misbehavior, appropriate to the age of the offender and without the strictures or adversarial nature of trial courts. By the same token, however, they weakened constitutional protections for children and families. Judges could incarcerate children without formally charging them with a crime, could hold them without due process, and, working closely with public schools, could subject them to supervision from other agencies, including welfare offices, detention halls, and psychiatric clinics. Meanwhile, the criteria for court involvement was maddeningly vague. Proceedings were often instigated by teachers and could move forward even over the objections of parents.[41]

It is important to underscore that not all children were equally subject to the effects of curricular tracking, shadowy record keeping, or court involvement; often, these mechanisms merely put a stamp of neutrality on existing inequalities. Boys were more likely to be swept up by the penal system than girls, and students experiencing poverty, students with disabilities, and students of color bore the brunt of segregation, surveillance, and coercion. Black children in particular confronted naked racism in the schools. Millions of Black families fled the South between the 1910s and 1950s, arriving in Northern cities where they continued to face housing restrictions, employment discrimination, and ghettoized schools with gerrymandered attendance zones and an inequitable distribution of funding and staffing. Alleged misbehavior by Black students was often the result of implicit (or not-so-implicit) bias from a majority-White teaching force. As one group of Black educators pointed out, when Black students' behavior records "tend to be at least half an inch thicker than those of white children . . . [it] tells you something about the child even before you open the folder," initiating a prejudicial cycle of punishment.[42] The historian Tera Agyepong notes multiple ways in which White teachers in Chicago mislabeled—and in the process criminalized—Black students' basic assertions of individuality. In a typical case, a boy named Harold Cobbs, newly arrived from Georgia, was sent to juvenile court for "behavioral problems." Although his teacher acknowledged that he was a strong student, she testified that he was "'incorrigible,' 'very persistently unruly,' 'dull,' 'energetic,' and 'ill-tempered.'" On that basis alone, and without his parents' consent, he was committed to a detention facility. Chicago justified such placements with support from the Institute for Juvenile Research, a psychiatric research center that diagnosed troubled youth. Black parents rejected the institute's research—rightly suspicious "that their race [was being] exploited by psychologists who used test results to prove something about the inferiority of Negro children"—but the practice of pathologizing Black students became routine, tightening a disciplinary nexus between psychological professionals, public schools, and juvenile courts. Even well-meaning educators subjected children to imprisonment. In another case, a Chicago principal had a boy committed for truancy despite his perfect attendance. The real problem was that the boy's parents were neglectful, which, in her view, made the state reform school a more wholesome alternative. "Something should be done," she cautioned, "to keep him off the streets and away from bad company." Here again, the appearance of bureaucratic order masked the exercise of arbitrary and discriminatory practices. In a city that made few provisions for the health or safety of Black children, even gestures of paternalism had to play out through the criminal justice system.[43]

Racial discrimination was often manifested through outright violence. Even as corporal punishment declined in the nation as a whole, Black students were subject to physical correction at far higher rates than their peers. Often wielding the belts and paddles were White teachers who freely described their students as "niggers," "pickaninnies," and "trash," baselessly claimed that these students were "more excitable" and "harder to handle," and made references to their moral and intellectual inferiority. When parents complained about such treatment, White principals dismissed them as liars or hysterics, asserting professional prerogative to keep order in the classroom.[44] Thus, while civil rights groups protested discriminatory punishment as early as the 1920s, forty years later Jonathan Kozol could still open his educational exposé, *Death at an Early Age* (1968), with the image of Black students being whipped in school basements.[45]

Racially disproportionate rates of punishment worsened in the aftermath of racial desegregation during the 1960s and 1970s.[46] Across the country, desegregation fomented student unrest, as slurs and physical attacks against students of color led to protests and retributive violence. White flight shrank tax bases in urban districts, leaving infrastructure in shambles and further undermining public confidence in the schools. "Smashed windows, fist fights, sit-ins and boycotts make the headlines," noted one contemporary report, "but the friction and disappointment that irritate students from day to day are rarely reported. Not until the lid blows off do parents and the public recognize that a precarious condition exists."[47] Within the classroom, many White educators treated minority students with a mixture of apathy and hostility. As an observer in Chicago put it, "When the Jewish students left South Shore High School and the blacks moved in, black teachers there saw white teachers who used to teach, cease to teach. They heard white teachers make statements such as, 'I used to be able to teach.' . . . And they made those statements with the clear implication that there was something wrong with the kids."[48] The trope of "uneducable" Black children compounded the mutual suspicion between Black students and parents on one side and teachers on the other, a breakdown of trust that led many educators to take a "hands-off" attitude toward discipline. "Rather than disciplining and counseling students in the classrooms, halls, and playgrounds," actions that they saw as futile, "teachers became reporters of violations for which the usual punishment was suspension or expulsion . . . [alienating] teachers from students who needed their counseling most." Unwilling to bridge the racial divide, educators turned outside the classroom for disciplinary support.[49] For their part, administrators took an increasingly hard-line stance toward student misbehavior. Principal Joe Clark became a national celebrity for carrying a baseball bat around the halls of his high school in Paterson, New Jersey, where he summarily expelled troublesome students.[50] The American Federation of Teachers, which represented educators in many urban areas, successfully lobbied for the preservation or reintroduction of corporal punishment in several cities, including Los Angeles and Miami. "Teachers want to maintain a healthy atmosphere and they need options," claimed a union representative.[51]

Most consequential was the introduction of police officers into public schools. Between the 1930s and the 1950s, as compulsory attendance became universal and the public became increasingly concerned with juvenile delinquency, some urban police departments came to see the school as a natural point of contact and crime prevention. Programs devoted to dialogue between teenagers and the police laid the groundwork for the "school resource officer" (SRO), a uniformed patrolman stationed within the school building.[52] As with juvenile courts, the presence of SROs was touted as preventative and even pedagogical: policemen would become role models and friendly authorities for troubled children, able to intervene more constructively in the hallway than they could on the street. These assumptions ignored some obvious conflicts of interest. SROs remained employees of the criminal justice system, meaning that friendly discipline could quickly slide toward arrest and court involvement. Confrontations between students and officers also introduced new standards of physicality. Although many schools still administered corporal punishment, the fact that a student could be wrestled to the ground or handcuffed to a chair by an armed man—and could face criminal penalties for resisting—was a new development. New privacy concerns arose as well. Did officers have the right to search children's belongings at a public school? Could they strip-search a child's body? Could they coerce confessions without a parent or a lawyer present? Could students incriminate themselves with passing remarks, and what information could officers share with their colleagues in the department? Underlying all of these issues was a lack of any meaningful training for officers themselves, who could act on their own simplistic understandings of child development and comportment.[53]

SRO programs, operating only in select schools during the 1950s, became more widespread following the student uprisings of the 1960s and 1970s. Most districts concentrated these positions in attendance zones with large numbers of Black and Latino students, even when crime statistics pointed to equal or greater rates of drug use, vandalism, and sexual assault in Whiter, suburban schools.[54] An important but often overlooked aspect of this story is the extent to which the growing police presence in schools was subsidized by state and federal anti-poverty funds. Even large school districts struggled to pay for security personnel with local taxes alone, and when the federal government allocated money for urban renewal during the mid-1960s, districts seized the opportunity to enlarge their budgets. Funding came from programs for juvenile delinquency prevention and workforce development in the Department of Health, Education, and Welfare; from the newly created Office of Law Enforcement Assistance, which expanded budgets and subsidized equipment for local police departments; and even from the Labor Department, which used the Emergency Employment Act (1971) to place unemployed men and women in public agencies like schools. Troublingly, some districts repurposed money intended for teaching positions in order to hire more security guards.[55] As these funds began to expire during the 1970s, state legislatures filled the gap, passing their own "safe school" acts to provide security equipment and personnel. Many of these laws included "zero tolerance" clauses, mandating automatic suspension for students in possession of drugs or weapons, and also for nebulous categories of disruption or disrespect.[56]

By the mid-1970s, then, with the number of suspensions climbing rapidly, it had become clear that the professionalization of schools had not achieved the sort of nurturing discipline that nineteenth-century reformers had hoped for. Structures designed to maintain order invoked the language of specialization but remained reliant on methods of force and exclusion, violating the special characteristics of schooling. The entire system seemed incapable of measured response, criminalizing the very children it was supposed to reform. The waning legitimacy of education officials prompted advocates of fair punishment to turn outside the system for redress: specifically, to state and federal courts.

The Campaign for Students' Rights

From the 1890s to the 1960s, courts increasingly authorized the use of police power, the state's right to govern children in the name of public welfare even in the face of parental objections. Whereas public education had once been rooted in common law, with families retaining significant control over the terms of their children's enrollment and course of study, the enforcement of compulsory attendance laws encouraged greater deference to school administrators in areas of curriculum, student placement, and discipline. Thus, for the first half of the twentieth century there was a marked trend away from student and family rights and toward a more encompassing vision of schooling. These changes did not reduce children to "mere creature[s] of the state," but they certainly strengthened the hand of teachers and administrators in their upbringing, including in the administration of punishment.[57] By the middle of the twentieth century, schools in most states could still spank children with impunity. Where corporal punishment had been abolished, suspensions and expulsions were on the rise. As noted above, schools cooperated closely with children's courts and welfare agencies, with little regard for legal representation or due process.[58] Abuses of these policies eventually prompted a critical review of the culture of professionalization and its relation to punishment: the centralization of school governance, education's compulsory nature, and its increasing influence on life outcomes made it difficult for courts to defer wholly to local districts in disciplinary matters. Teachers were gaining new legal protections—including protections from arbitrary dismissal, and rights to association and free speech—and the degree to which students enjoyed corresponding constitutional rights became a signal question.[59] Courts took some steps to establish children's rights during the late 1960s and early 1970s, but schools' special status as pedagogical and ostensibly open institutions made judges hesitant to jeopardize classroom order or limit the purportedly educational purposes of punishment.

We agree that schools should be orderly, that punishment should be educative, and that judges should defer to elected officials whenever possible. However, we also contend that superficial endorsement of these goals or failure to recognize the institutional contexts in which they play out can produce poor legal reasoning and perpetuate injustice under the guise of sound principle.[60] In this case, by ignoring the increasingly bureaucratic administration of school punishment, state and federal courts produced a case law built on some highly tenuous conclusions. Prominent legal scholars now argue that in "no arena of education law is there greater need for renewed attention than in assessing how schools sanction wayward students," and we heartily support that claim.[61]

The 1960s witnessed a revolution in the rights of accused adults, most famously with the guarantee of publicly funded legal representation in *Gideon v. Wainwright* (1963) and the enumeration of due process rights during an arrest in *Miranda v. Arizona* (1966).[62] Juvenile justice reform seemed to follow a parallel course. Confronted with cases involving habeas corpus and due process claims outside of school, judges found that courts could not arbitrarily reclassify children as adults (*Kent v. United States* [1966]) and had to notify parents and offer hearings before sweeping children into juvenile detention (*In re Gault* [1967]).[63] These decisions weakened the government's ability to assert custody of minors and allowed children to enter the adversarial legal process as full participants, reining in the discretion of judges and caseworkers. By the end of the decade, federal courts proved willing to intervene in disciplinary decisions within schools as well. Whereas courts had previously deferred to the decisions of teachers and administrators on almost all questions of classroom order, in *Tinker v. Des Moines* (1969), a landmark recognition of student speech rights, the US Supreme Court invalidated the suspension of a group of students who wore armbands to protest military action in Vietnam. "Students don't shed their constitutional rights to freedom of speech or expression at the schoolhouse gates," the justices famously stated.[64] Nevertheless, the schoolhouse did have a function to perform, and the preservation of order remained a limiting factor. In *Tinker*, the majority specifically noted that the Iowa protests did not involve "disruptive action or even group demonstrations," and that while "a few students made hostile remarks to the students wearing armbands, there were no threats or acts of violence on school premises." Only when students framed their protests respectfully and maturely and their classmates and teachers responded in kind could they rely on constitutional protections.[65]

Even when confronted with unruly behavior, courts began to accord students some rights, and it is here that they reviewed disciplinary practices most directly. In 1971, Black teenagers in Columbus, Ohio, galvanized by the cancellation of Black History Week, decided to protest ongoing racism in their schools. At Central High School, a group interrupted a class meeting in the auditorium and (indirectly) incited property destruction in the cafeteria. School administrators summarily suspended seventy-five students, informing them of the reason after the fact or not at all. In *Goss v. Lopez* (1975), the Supreme Court found that doing so violated students' due process rights. Again, the decision used measured language. "Some modicum of discipline and order is essential if the educational function is to be performed," Justice Byron White wrote for the majority. "Events calling for discipline are frequent occurrences, and sometimes require immediate, effective action. Suspension is considered not only to be a necessary tool to maintain order, but a valuable educational device." At the same time, granting unchecked authority to school officials could undermine punishment's educational significance. "It would be a strange disciplinary system," White continued, "if no communication was sought by the disciplinarian with the student in an effort to inform him of his dereliction and to let him tell his side of the story in order to make sure that an injustice is not done." Especially since several students pleaded their innocence, the administration owed the students an opportunity to answer the accusations being made against them.[66] Here White invoked the expressive theory of punishment that we discussed in chapter 1. If punishment is a form of dialogue between the community and an offender, unexplained judgments from afar deny the accused an opportunity to explain or repent, at the same time rendering the sanctions incoherent and thus meaningless.

Not all the justices agreed with that logic. In a sharply worded dissent, Justice Lewis Powell argued that school suspensions did not merit judicial review at all and that he could find no basis for "federal courts, rather than educational officials and state legislatures . . . to determine the rules applicable to routine classroom discipline of children and teenagers in the public schools." Essentially, Powell claimed that ruling in the students' favor would tie the hands of teachers and administrators, jeopardizing school order with procedural requirements for even the smallest forms of correction.[67] Conservative critics have echoed these concerns ever since, blaming *Lopez* for introducing unworkable disciplinary systems into schools and undermining sanctioned authority. Yet theirs is a tenuous line of argument, mostly because the decision's interpretation of "due process" is so minimal. *Lopez* did not require the involvement of lawyers or even parents in disciplinary hearings; an informal conversation between the disciplinarian and the student would satisfy its requirements. Indeed, the case merely affirmed what most schools were doing anyway. To whatever degree schools did adopt bureaucratic disciplinary structures, those structures predated *Lopez* and were products of the rationalization and professionalism referenced above.

More notable, in hindsight, was the court's facile acceptance of suspensions themselves, which rose sharply in the years surrounding the case—not coincidentally, the peak era of racial desegregation. White based his support for due process rights on the speculation that suspension might damage a student's reputation or "interfere with later opportunities for higher education and employment," a claim that Powell ridiculed as utterly ungrounded in evidence. Powell countered that "absences of such limited duration will rarely affect a pupil's opportunity to learn or his scholastic performance" and therefore should *not* implicate due process, making a statement that was itself utterly ungrounded in evidence. Subsequent studies have shown that White was much closer to the truth and, if anything, had underestimated the impact of suspensions, which have determinative effects not only on the school completion of individual students but also on the academic attainment of entire schools, and remain racially disproportionate in their application.[68]

Powell's comments underscore several interrelated weaknesses in arguments supporting school punishment that were made during the 1970s. First, attempts to seem levelheaded could lead to unquestioned acceptance of an unjust status quo. Powell's speculation that hearings for short-term suspensions would leave "school authorities [with] time to do little else" avoided the question of why schools relied so heavily on suspensions in the first place, not to mention whether ten days in fact constituted a "short-term" suspension. Powell repeatedly sought to minimize the punishments in the case, noting that the verdict would apply equally to one-day suspensions and then using the smaller number throughout his dissent. Doing so allowed him to present schools as quasi-sacred spaces in which punishments were lenient, local voters exercised meaningful oversight, and the state and the student had congruent interests, making procedural protections unnecessary. That interpretation may have been appealing in principle but bore little resemblance to the increasingly bureaucratic and persistently discriminatory schools of the era. Moreover, it is hard to credit Powell's earnest statements about school's significance when he so flippantly dismissed the effect of punishment on students. How important could an institution be if separation from it "leaves no scars; affects no reputations; indeed . . . often may be viewed by the young as a badge of some distinction and a welcome holiday"?[69]

The shortcomings of Powell's nostalgia came into sharper focus just two years later, when he wrote the majority opinion in *Ingraham v. Wright* (1977). In that case, James Ingraham, a Black teenager from a junior high school in Florida, was brought to the principal's office for disrupting an assembly. The principal, William Wright, also Black, told Ingraham that he would get five swats from a wooden paddle. Ingraham denied any wrongdoing. Wright heatedly ordered two other administrators to hold the boy's arms and legs and proceeded to strike him more than twenty times. Ingraham suffered a blood mass, for which he was hospitalized and kept out of school for more than a week. Other students testified that the same administrators patrolled the hall with wooden paddles, regularly beat students, threw them against walls, hit them with belt buckles, and struck them on the head and neck if they resisted, causing injuries for which they, too, had been hospitalized. Ingraham and his parents sued the district, alleging that the school had violated the Eighth Amendment's prohibition of "cruel and unusual" punishment and the Fourteenth Amendment's protections of due process and equal protection of the law.[70] On appeal, the US Supreme Court rejected their petition and affirmed state and local responsibility to set disciplinary policy, including corporal punishment, restrained only by significant changes to public opinion, which the justices could not find.[71]

The decision leaned heavily on Powell's earlier dissent in *Lopez*. First, the decision noted courts' traditional deference to school officials on matters of discipline, which, for Powell, justified almost any sort of punishment. "Paddling of recalcitrant children has long been an accepted method of promoting good behavior," he wrote. It provided a way to instill "notions of responsibility and decorum into the mischievous heads of school children." The decision claimed that the ban on "cruel and unusual" punishment applied only to criminals, on the basis of their formal conviction and subjugation to a prison environment. Because schools were open institutions, in which students spent only part of the day and over which communities exercised some oversight, they were not subject to the same prohibitions. Powell briefly acknowledged the troubling nature of Ingraham's accusations—which seemed to indicate that the school had flouted Florida's own standard of "degrading or unduly severe" punishment and its formal reporting requirements—but the court declined to evaluate the case on the basis of substantive due process, narrowing its findings to whether corporal punishment was an Eighth Amendment violation and whether, as in *Goss v. Lopez*, punishment required disciplinary hearings or parental notification. Powell noted that cases of abuse were outliers in the general application of physical punishment. "Because paddlings are usually inflicted in response to conduct directly observed by teachers in their presence," he wrote, "the risk that a child will be paddled without cause is typically insignificant." Nor did corporal punishment merit the disciplinary hearings required under *Lopez*, Powell claimed, since any formal requirement would be "less than a fair-minded principal would impose on himself." He suggested that if abuse were to occur, as it had in this case, students could seek redress through civil lawsuits and state law.[72]

Again, this ruling relied on dubious legal logic. It was true that courts had historically deferred to legislatures on the issue of corporal punishment, but they usually did so with less relish and with stricter standards of scrutiny than Powell himself had. As early as the 1850s, state and federal courts lamented that "the public [seemed] to cling to a despotism in the government of schools which has been discarded everywhere else," and resolved that until legislation changed, they could at least judge "every case strictly within the rule [and] hold the unworthy perpetrator guilty of assault and battery" in the face of extreme punishment.[73] Writing the dissent in *Ingraham*, Justice White reached a similar conclusion. "If the Eighth Amendment does not bar moderate spanking in public schools," he wrote, "it is because moderate spanking is not 'cruel and unusual,' not because it is not 'punishment' as the majority suggests." To overstate the special status of schools was to put an arbitrary limit on judicial review. "If a punishment is so barbaric and inhumane that it goes beyond the tolerance of a civilized society," White continued, "its openness to public scrutiny should have nothing to do with its constitutional validity." Likewise, Powell's suggestion that students could seek justice through state courts was mistaken. First, because "the availability of state remedies has never been determinative of the coverage or of the protections afforded by the Eighth Amendment"; second, because redress after the fact was unable to heal the wounds that children suffered; and most of all because several states, including Florida, granted statutory immunity to teachers who claimed to act in good faith, to the point that only *permanent physical injury* to a child would constitute a criminal violation.[74]

The last point illustrates the distance between Powell's image of nurturing disciplinarians and the reality of the ways in which schools were actually insulated from the influence of local communities and individual parents. Powell himself noted that while "early cases viewed the authority of the teacher as deriving from the parents, the concept of parental delegation has been replaced by the view—more consonant with compulsory education laws—that the State itself may impose such corporal punishment as is reasonably necessary."[75] Nineteenth-century courts upheld the school's right to strike children over parental objections, but they did so in an era when educational governance was local and attendance was more or less voluntary. Unremarked on were the ways in which compulsory attendance and subjection to state governance should have formalized the safeguards against abuse, or the possibility that state-sanctioned punishment could implicate other, more recent constitutional rights, such as racial nondiscrimination. Powell's account of school punishment bore only tenuous resemblance to the past and to his contemporary context in the 1970s, which witnessed tens of thousands of reported incidents of corporal punishment each year, among them dozens of cases of children being cuffed, thrown into walls, and hospitalized after beatings.[76] One boy had his head slammed into the bleachers for refusing to do extra push-ups.[77] Another was knocked unconscious for swearing at an administrator.[78] When a group of nine-year-olds dawdled in gym class, their teacher tied them behind his motorcycle and dragged them through the parking lot.[79] A female high school student in Texas remembered administrators rubbing the paddle on her bottom before striking it, "an exercise in pornographic amusement for the perpetrators."[80] In Louisiana, a sixth-grade teacher regularly whipped students with a length of garden hose. In Illinois, a middle school teacher used a battery-powered cattle prod.[81] *Ingraham* gave lower courts no guidance to curb these incidents and, by ignoring the realities of administrative bureaucracy, did nothing to reclaim the moral standing that Powell valued in schools.[82]

In the decade after *Ingraham*, federal appeals courts took up substantive due process claims on their own and did establish *some* limits on corporal punishment. In *Hall v. Tawney* (1980), in which an elementary school student was struck by a metal drawer divider, and *Garcia v. Miera* (1987), in which a nine-year-old girl was held upside down and beaten bloody across the front of her thighs, appellate courts found that educators' actions sufficiently "shocked the conscience" to implicate substantive due process and put excessive punishment beyond the bounds of law.[83] However, these decisions provided only gradual and incomplete relief. For one thing, the timing of rulings varied between circuits. (The United States Court of Appeals for the Fifth Circuit, which encompasses Texas, Louisiana, and Mississippi, has still not established any rights against excessive punishment.)[84] Meanwhile, as courts and state legislatures expanded qualified immunity for public employees, safeguarding them not merely from civil suits but also from criminal charges, it became far more difficult to bring teachers and administrators to trial. In cases without ironclad evidence, those in which existing law was indeterminate, or those in which educators claimed to follow districts' formal procedures, courts had to summarily dismiss charges.[85] The vague wording of district disciplinary policies could justify all sorts of harsh treatment, which was another way that the bureaucratization of schools protected teachers at the expense of students. And even when especially egregious forms of punishment resulted in rulings for students, the consequent precedents could implicitly sanction less serious but still abusive forms of punishment. As we noted in chapter 1, there are still over 150,000 children a year being physically punished in America's public schools, often in ways that remain legally suspect. To take one example, Jessica Serafin, an eighteen-year-old in San Antonio, Texas, left her high school campus to get breakfast and returned before the tardy bell. However, for violating the school's "closed campus" rule, she was struck with a four-foot-long piece of wood, leaving her bottom bloodied and her hand swollen. Serafin sued the district for battery but lost at the district and appellate levels. The circuit court ruled that corporal punishment "is only a deprivation of substantive due process rights 'when it is arbitrary, capricious, or wholly unrelated to the legitimate state goal of maintaining an atmosphere conducive to learning,'" and pointed out that Texas had statutes to prevent abuse. As in so many other cases, though, the court made no inquiry into whether the school complied with those statutes.[86]

Like Justice Powell, we envision schools as places of legitimate authority and shared moral commitments. However, we find corporal punishment inconsistent with that goal, for both ethical and legal reasons.

When it comes to the ethics of punishment, we find striking children objectionable on a number of grounds. There is, in some cases, serious bodily damage that can come from such punishment—cuts, bruises, and worse.[87] There is also a mental toll. Many studies have found that physical punishment in children is associated with later mood disorders, anxiety disorders, substance abuse, and personality disorders.[88] There are also serious worries about what this form of punishment does to the classroom environment and to the trusting relationships that should exist between educators and students. One might ask whether proper educational relationships are possible under an ever-present threat of being physically beaten. The historical record, as we have seen, is full of harrowing accounts of schools disrupted by violent punishments. In a recent report from Human Rights Watch, we see similar dynamics in modern-day schooling. One teacher described how physical punishment would interrupt her mathematics class: "We'd be in the middle of math class and we'd hear a crack [in the next room]."[89] The report also quotes a high school student describing how corporal punishment would impact the school environment: "I didn't see it but I could hear it. Licks would be so loud and hard you could hear it through the walls. You could hear the moans and yelling through the walls."[90] It is worth asking, of course, whether learning can proceed effectively in such a context.

Beyond the disturbing interruption of academic activities, there are messages of power and violence that are sent through such punishment. Here, again, we should make a distinction between the expressive function of punishment and what is expressed by any particular punishment, the "secondary expression." The expressive message of corporal punishment goes beyond what is sent with other forms of punishment. It seems to endorse physical violence as a solution to problems and establishes the precedent that "might makes right." Corporal punishment validates physical violence in human life. There is some psychological research supporting the idea that this message is sent and received. One study found that adolescents engaged in more violent behaviors, like bullying and fighting, when their parents used physical punishment at home.[91]

There is also historical evidence that physical punishment taps into alarming emotions on the part of adults. Corporal punishment can become an exercise in power, producing a disturbing tolerance for, or even pleasure in, the suffering of others. As we have seen, educators in the past sometimes reflected on themselves when they administered corporal punishment and, looking in the mirror, did not like what they saw. Corporal punishment can be corruptive of teachers' self-concept. For these reasons, corporal punishment is indeed a practice that demands careful scrutiny.

There is a different set of legal objections to corporal punishment. While we consider ethical implications of paramount importance to educators and citizens, we recognize that they are not binding in courts. Judges are rightly moved by standards of evidence and precedent, and their inexpert reliance on philosophy or social science can produce poor judicial reasoning.[92] Likewise, it is important to emphasize that American courts are not beholden to vaguely defined cultural norms nor to international prohibitions on corporal punishment, such as the United Nations' Convention on the Rights of the Child (1989). While it may seem troubling that the United States is the only nation in the world not to sign that document—the result of long-standing resistance to encroachment on national or family sovereignty—it is hardly the only nation that allows teachers to strike their students. Beating school-children remains legal in sixty-nine countries and was only formally prohib-ited in many nations after the year 2000. The United States is often compared unfavorably to Europe, which has uniformly outlawed corporal punishment in its schools, but might be better judged against countries with strong pro-vincial or territorial governments (such as Australia, which has a patchwork of regulations for government and nongovernment schools), those with sig-nificant cultural divides between rural areas and urban areas (as in many Latin American nations and Asian nations, where physical punishment prac-tices remain entrenched in the countryside), or those with histories of set-tler colonialism and racist violence (such as Brazil and South Africa).[93] In these cases, the contrast is somewhat less clear. Some countries have made the abolition of corporal punishment a cornerstone of their postcolonial iden-tity, moving away from the practice far more purposefully than the United States; others persist in forms of casual violence that would be unacceptable in any American school. All this is to say that legacies of authoritarian teach-ing are not uniquely American, and while symbolic commitment to the rights of the child may count for something, many democracies have struggled to bring rhetorical commitments in line with their practices, one more reason that international norms are not especially helpful in critiquing American jurisprudence.

Nor do we mean to impugn the notion of judicial restraint within the American political system itself: federal judges cannot solve all issues of edu-cational policy, and it is possible that sporadic acts of violence do not rise to the level of constitutional violation. Under current jurisprudence, civil rights claims invoking the Fourteenth Amendment are subject to one of two tests. If the state has infringed a fundamental right enumerated in the Constitution or targeted a "suspect class" on the basis of race, religion, or other protected characteristics, federal courts subject the case to "strict scrutiny," demand-ing a compelling reason to uphold the state's action. Compelling reasons are hard to find, making this standard "strict in theory and fatal in fact," almost always favoring the plaintiff.[94] If the case does not involve a fundamental right or a suspect class, however, courts apply a "rational basis" test, asking only whether the law in question is reasonably related to a legitimate state inter-est. Courts take the broadest possible view of rational action. They do not require legislatures to clarify their intention in passing a law, for example, and will often substitute hypothetical justifications for the actual facts of the case. Making every attempt to defer to elected officials, rational basis renders judicial scrutiny "virtually nonexistent." Deciding which standard to apply, then, essentially predetermines the outcomes of these cases.[95]

Defenders of judicial restraint have traditionally favored rational basis, the lower standard of scrutiny, as a safeguard of democratic deliberation and a brake on the unwieldy expansion of protected rights. Regarding school punishment, they argue that any heightened scrutiny of disciplinary policy will hamstring local officials, jeopardizing order and safety. We disagree. From our perspective, such claims grossly oversimplify the options open to state and federal courts and, paradoxically, have themselves inhibited public deliberation about school punishment.[96]

The bifurcated approach to equal protection often seems ill-suited to issues of educational policy. Although it has been established that education is not a fundamental right and that schoolchildren are not a suspect class, the Supreme Court has repeatedly equivocated on those issues. *Brown v. Board of Education* (1954), for instance, argued that education "is a right which must be made available to all on equal terms," and while *San Antonio v. Rodriguez* (1973) curtailed that claim—finding that education was not enumerated in the US Constitution, and thus that constitutional law did not guarantee equal funding of public schools—even *Rodriguez* conceded that some degree of inequality would constitute a rights violation.[97] In *Plyler v. Doe* (1982), which overturned a state law denying undocumented immigrants a free public education, the court raised the possibility of a third approach. In that case, the dissenting justices complained that the majority established a "quasi-suspect-class" and "quasi-fundamental-rights" to education, applying an intermediate standard between strict scrutiny and rational basis, which the dissenters worried would invite subjectivity and overreach in future decisions.[98]

We would argue, to the contrary, that intermediate scrutiny is exactly what is called for. By applying judgment to the facts at hand, courts are able to weigh individual rights against state interests in more nuanced ways, resulting in narrower decisions and the possibility of dialogue between courts, local governments, and the public.[99] Intermediate scrutiny also allows federal judges to engage colleagues at the state level without upsetting judicial federalism.[100] This was precisely the virtue of Justice White's dissent in *Ingraham v. Wright*. Rather than issuing a sweeping judgment on all forms of corporal punishment, as the majority did, White tailored a narrower indictment of an obviously abusive example of the practice. In recent decades, the same approach has successfully controlled decisions in other areas of educational policy, particularly around questions of race and gender in university admissions. In these instances, federal judges have not usurped the judgment of local administrators but, through serious consideration of the facts at hand, have impelled them to develop more rigorous procedures to safeguard student rights.[101] State courts have also begun to subject educational laws (especially funding formulas) to more stringent forms of "rational basis" review, in which they have found patterns of inequality arbitrary and indefensible.[102]

The same standards could be profitably applied to the issue of corporal punishment, which certainly implicates "quasi-fundamental" rights of racial and gender bias, as well as more explicit questions of substantive due process. Whatever one thinks about the physical punishment of schoolchildren, in case after case there has been no proportional relationship between the penalty and the alleged misbehavior, no demand that districts prove the efficacy of their methods, nor any serious consideration of states' self-imposed limits on teacher behavior.

We largely agree with the sociologist Richard Arum that school discipline over the past fifty years has suffered from an increase in court supervision and the attendant rise of bureaucratic formalism, a process "that proved destructive of school moral authority yet failed to ameliorate racial and socioeconomic disparities in disciplinary outcomes."[103] Judges should not micromanage disciplinary practices in schools, which are rightly the purview of teachers and school boards, nor should they seek to establish an inflexible set of student rights, which at any rate they have endorsed inconsistently and conditionally. However, because Arum sees rulings for student rights as the *cause* of these changes—arguing that the threat of lawsuits has inhibited professional discretion and moral legitimacy—he finds judicial scrutiny almost uniformly undesirable. Taking a longer view, we think that the courts still have a role to play. It was school systems themselves, not courts, that leached punishment of its moral overtones, stifled public oversight, and systematized inequality in service of a superficial professionalism, and they did so well before the 1960s. Thus, from *Ingraham* to the present, the fundamental choice is not whether courts will expand the scope of student rights by fiat or preserve a flawed but serviceable system of state and local decision-making, but whether they will challenge school districts to earn the legitimacy that they claim. As it stands, the Supreme Court's unwillingness to distinguish between degrees of punishment has allowed appellate and state courts, legislatures, and school boards to follow suit, holding states beneath their own constitutional standards and denying the public a basis for serious judgment. In circular fashion, it was the oversight of exactly these institutions that Justice Powell took for granted when he exempted schools from the Eighth Amendment. Absent a strong statement from the judiciary, it seems that the boundaries of school punishment will be determined by public prejudice or by bureaucratic imperatives, neither of which advances philosophically sound solutions.

Origins of the School-to-Prison Pipeline

During the 1990s, political theorists William Bennett, John DiIulio, and John Walter extrapolated existing crime statistics to warn about a rising genera- tion of "radically impulsive, brutally remorseless youngsters," a group they described as "superpredators."[104] The authors attributed the coming horde to the "moral poverty" of American society—by then a common complaint— and argued that welfare programs were insufficient to overcome family dys- function or attenuated community relations. To their credit, they rejected the fallacy that tougher sentencing would act as a deterrent: without a strong moral basis, government sanction would be just as ineffective as government support.[105] Yet, predictably, that nuance was lost amid their fearmongering, and when Congress passed the Violent Crime Control and Law Enforce- ment Act (1994) and the Gun-Free Schools Act (1994), it instituted exactly the sort of punitive regime that Bennett, DiIulio, and Walter warned against. The crime control act introduced the so-called "three strikes" laws for adults, swelling prison populations with primarily nonviolent offenders. The Gun- Free Schools Act, drawing from state-level legislation, expanded "zero toler- ance" policies in schools, which initially applied to the possession of weapons or drugs but soon spread to a variety of other transgressions, from cutting class to use of belligerent language. Suspensions skyrocketed.[106]

Suspension and corporal punishment remain the most significant prob- lems confronting school discipline today, and the issue of racial inequality— lurking at the margins of *Goss v. Lopez* and *Ingraham v. Wright*—has recently taken center stage. Beginning at already disproportionate levels, suspension rates have nearly doubled for non-White students since the 1970s, jumping from 6 percent to 15 percent for Black students, but only from 3 percent to 4.8 percent for White students. In middle school, where the trend is most pronounced, at least 175 districts suspend more than 33 percent of their Black male students, and 95 districts suspend the same proportion of Black female students. This should be troubling to all who are concerned with equality and racial justice, even if disparities in student discipline, "taken alone, do not establish whether unlawful discrimination has occurred."[107]

It is likely that there are several different causes for this "discipline gap." Some of the proposed explanations for disproportionate rates of punishment include poverty and neighborhood characteristics, low academic achieve- ment, differential behavior, differential selection in the students singled out for punishment, and differential processing of individual cases.[108] In reality, the discipline gap is likely a combination of many different factors. Some of the proposed explanations, though, are more plausible than others. One possible explanation, for example, is based on socioeconomic class. Students raised in poverty are, on average, less academically prepared and more likely to experience trauma at home, and therefore more likely to have trouble in school. Proponents of this theory claim that the punishment discrepancy is based on the behavior of these students who are not as prepared for school and not on something like racial bias. It just so happens that the percentage of Black students experiencing poverty is higher than that of White students, they claim.[109] Max Eden of the conservative Manhattan Institute, for example, has argued that the disparities are better explained in terms of a student's socioeconomic status and family makeup than in terms of racial discrimination. "What we're seeing here is huge inequities in American society reflected in these numbers," Eden said to the *Washington Post*. "It's not the school as an institution that's responsible for it."[110] In this view, disparities in punishment grow out of social inequalities, and schools are simply responding to these larger forces.

Data showing the persistence of the disparity when class is accounted for, however, demonstrate that this explanation is inadequate. For example, one summary of the research on racial disparities concludes, "Multivariate studies controlling for socioeconomic status have consistently found that Black-White differences in out-of-school suspension persist regardless of controls for poverty; that is, while Black students in the most extreme poverty situations are more likely than their White peers to be suspended, Black students are overrepresented in suspension across the rest of the economic spectrum as well."[111] Black students coming from similar class backgrounds as White students are still punished more frequently and more severely. While class does matter, this argument against the presence of racial discrimination is not supported by the available evidence.

Another explanation is that Black students are, by nature, less well-behaved and more aggressive than White students. According to this theory, Black students simply act out more than White students, which explains the difference in punishment. Any explanation based in such "natural differences" needs to be rejected for a number of reasons. First, in a society like the United States, with a long history of brutal and persistent racial discrimination, "natural" accounts of racial disparities should be viewed with heightened suspicion, whether a natural difference is alleged in aggression, intelligence, or anything else. This historical context and the continuing displays of overt racism recently seen in the United States suggest that our judgments about natural differences simply cannot be trusted and, thus, these sorts of "natural" explanations for social differences should be removed from the table for the foreseeable future.

Second, there is empirical data suggesting that bias is at work in applications of discipline and punishment, and that the different rates of punishment

across racial groups are not the product of objective assessment of school behavior. The following are just a few examples: One study found that research
participants perceive Black boys as being more responsible for their actions
than White boys of the same age. The authors of the study state, "We find
converging evidence that Black boys are seen as older and less innocent and
that they prompt a less essential conception of childhood than do their White
same-age peers."[112] Another study found that when shown videos that purportedly displayed student misbehavior, preschool teachers' eyes were drawn
more frequently to Black children than to White children, even though neither group was actually misbehaving.[113] Other studies have found that teachers reading about identical student infractions were more likely to judge as
"extreme" the behaviors that were connected to students with common Black
names. Teachers also saw infractions by students with typically Black names
as more interconnected, more reflective of the student's character, and thus
more likely to lead to suspension than identical histories of students with
typically White names. This leads us to the unavoidable conclusion that racial
bias partly underlies the racial disparity. Black students are punished more
often and more harshly than White students *for the same behavior*. And, indeed, studies of school disciplinary records tend to confirm this suspicion.[114]

Divergent accounts of racial disproportionality can significantly influence
one's understanding of the school-to-prison pipeline, in which children of
color are inexorably channeled toward the criminal justice system.[115] Some
critics have objected to the pipeline image as overly mechanistic.[116] Conservative writers argue that while students of color are more likely to be suspended
and then jailed, researchers have yet to establish a causal link between the
three variables or to account for their impact on individual students. Again,
they argue, the determinative factor might be poverty rather than race. If that
is the case, then attempts to address the problem by withholding federal funding from districts with racially disproportionate records of punishment—a
strategy pursued by the US Department of Education under President Barack
Obama, since reversed by the Trump administration—is the wrong solution
to the issue and bound to impose ineffective disciplinary policies onto the
schools. A few writers go further, stating that attempts at disciplinary reform
have already "recklessly morphed into de facto 'no student removal' policies"
and led to spikes in student violence and declining school climate.[117]

These points should challenge policy makers to refine assumptions about
the diagnosis and remediation of biased punishments. Conservatives are
probably right that a multifaceted issue like school discipline can be handled only imprecisely at the federal level, and they are certainly correct that
terminology remains slippery and that the issue remains undertheorized.[118]

Nevertheless, conservatives cannot deny that there is pervasive racial bias in school punishment and often rely on fallacies or misleading information in their attempts to do so. Some invert gaps in causal evidence, criticizing a lack of data while using the same uncertainty to advance their own speculative explanations, or leaning on a single fact to insinuate a larger ideological truth. For example, when some writers point out that students of color are not punished more harshly for the same offenses as White students, they immediately shift discussion to serious forms of misconduct like student violence, where rates of suspension are comparable.[119] In doing so, however, they elide the central assertion of the pipeline model, which is that for minor, subjective offenses like "disrespect," students of color *are* punished more harshly and more frequently, and that these minor incidents now account for the majority of suspensions.[120] Thus, while conservative critiques open possibilities for future research, they neither discredit the pipeline metaphor nor necessarily warrant their authors' conclusions.

There have also been some objections to the school-to-prison pipeline model from the Left. The sociologist Ken McGrew, for instance, points out multiple ways in which references to the pipeline as a phenomenon (rather than simply as a metaphor) obscure questions about its theoretical underpinnings and ideological implications. While the statistics around youth incarceration are troubling, he states, it is hardly the case that "the numbers speak for themselves."[121] McGrew finds that much of the scholarship around the school-to-prison pipeline accepts the amnesic proposition that it is a recent historical development, a product of the 1990s. As we have demonstrated throughout this chapter, it is not.[122] Likewise, existing literature tends to omit any broader discussion of political economy, which, as we established in the previous chapter, has always been inseparable from disciplinary structures. These omissions allow some proponents to suggest that the pipeline can simply be redirected from prison to college—that keeping children in school longer will necessarily improve their employment prospects and reduce the likelihood of later imprisonment without requiring changes in the economic systems that produce poverty and crime in the first place, an obviously suspect conclusion.[123] McGrew also argues that current scholarship tends to uncritically accept the pipeline as a tool of social reproduction, either downplaying or only selectively invoking the role of human agency in its function or in resistance to it.[124]

Conclusion

We would like to return attention to human agency as well—as a perpetuator of inequitable school punishments but also, perhaps, as their remedy. The central claim of this chapter has been that, since the early twentieth century, the rhetoric of professionalization has stripped punishment of its moral purpose, encouraging shallow references to child benefit while ruthlessly imposing efficiency and order. This was a narrow and, one might say, counterfeit vision of professionalism, in which educators separated punishment from teaching, offloading it first to administrators and then to the police. Where teachers continued to inflict punishment, procedural protections too easily excused unprofessional behavior and abuse. Meanwhile, schools refined older systems of control, implementing spatial segregation, intrusive testing, and (more recently) metal detectors and surveillance cameras. While physical punishment remains a possibility across much of the country, processes of standardization and supervision are more common than spanking.[125]

These measures deny human flourishing and, because they are subtle and less subject to criticism, they inhibit nuanced debate about the purpose of disciplinary policies. Reliance on federal or judicial oversight of school punishment may be necessary to some degree, but such oversight is bound to be generalized and oriented to minimal standards, most helpful as symbols or prompts for local debate and deliberation. Our position is that formalization has outsourced judgment, creating a system in which almost all participants can deny responsibility for unjust outcomes. Corporal punishment does not seem to be going anywhere. Suspensions are increasingly problematic. Yet courts and schools are not inclined to correct either without the same public pressure that professionalization has stifled. The logic of professionalization has promoted institutional stability over moral development, and frustrated attempts at public accountability.

These dynamics are nearing the point of absurdity. Teachers and researchers are again promoting therapeutic techniques, from mindfulness training and "grit" to sensory rooms and trauma-informed pedagogy. Each of these approaches foregrounds the emotional or sensory aspects of learning, and insofar as they foster self-mastery within students or increase sensitivity and respect from teachers, they may be salutary. If they are not embedded in a broader system of just punishment, however, they are meaningless. We opened this book with a few examples of the opposite side of school punishment, in which educators overreacted to childish behavior, administrators criminalized disability or racial identity, and police officers brutally subdued children. While these examples (and hundreds more like them) give the impression of a disciplinary system divorced from common sense, they also speak to the ongoing role of discretion in its administration. If individual disciplinary authority seems attenuated in public schools today, it is often because teachers and administrators have forfeited their responsibilities to bureaucratic policies; at the same time, if there are instances of overreach, it is because disciplinarians have chosen to exercise their prerogative. Studies find that the most expansive applications of "zero tolerance" policies occur at the local (rather than the state or federal) level and that a strong predictor of exclusionary discipline remains the attitude of individual school principals. Where principals question the necessity of suspension and expulsion, rates of these practices tend to be lower and preventative disciplinary programs tend to be more robust.[126] Such correlations do not mean that changing attitudes alone will end discriminatory punishment, but they do suggest that individual discussions about wisdom, judgment, trust, and the special characteristics of education could fruitfully replace images of a totalizing system of social control.[127] That is, engaging historical and philosophical questions at the local level could revive debates about the appropriate boundary between democratic authority and professional authority, and the ways in which each might be best suited to the discipline of children. Whether or not such discussions would produce radical change in the schools, they remain prerequisites for any moral and democratic system of discipline. Our goal in the final chapter is to outline our criteria for such a system and to present approaches that can make school punishment more just and workable.

Punishment and the Moral Community of Schools

We have surveyed the long and complex history of punishment in schools. Several issues from our historical account are worth highlighting. We saw an early emphasis on moral formation and strict classroom order, enforced through corporal punishment for those who misbehaved. Corporal punishment was generally (but not entirely) replaced by growing bureaucratic systems of student control. The moral discourse surrounding student punishment receded, exchanged for therapeutic languages and managerial strategies (often drawing from outside institutions like law enforcement) meant to keep school order and discipline. The rigid, heavy-handed moralism of early schools evolved into the morally sterile behavior-management clinics of later schools, with several associated pathologies, such as the school-to-prison pipeline. Neither approach, we believe, correctly recognizes the nature of schools as moral communities.

What is needed is a reconsideration of the nature of schooling, particularly of how we think of schools as communities governed by a set of values and moral norms. If we take schools seriously—not as rigid enforcers of authoritarian control or as managerial bureaucracies, but as moral communities—what then follows for punishment practices? Our goal is to give serious consideration to what this shift in perspective might tell us about how students should interact with one another, how educators should interact with students, and how schools should interact with larger communities. A clear conception of the nature of schools as moral communities will unlock the proper conception of discipline and punishment.

Our task then is to describe the proper moral community of schools. At first, though, it is not entirely clear how this is supposed to be done. On what grounds do we stipulate not simply what school communities currently are but also what they *should* be? It is not obvious how a normative vision of school community can be achieved such that it can attain some degree of social consensus. One way to think about the moral nature of schools, we suggest, is to consider what makes them unique as social institutions. We can ask what goals schools are striving toward, what obstacles they face in achieving those goals, and what is necessary to overcome those obstacles. The sorts of discipline practices and the sorts of social relationships that should exist within schools will depend on the specific institutional context of schools, properly described. In short, the context of schools, *as schools*, matters.

The Ethical Importance of School Context

Before describing the context of schooling more specifically, we should note the role of institutional context in ethical deliberation. When we think of the moral responsibilities of citizens within liberal democracies, we often tend to think in terms of universal rights and obligations—broad-based rights such as freedoms of speech and association, rights to due process, and rights to equality of treatment under the law. While such universal rights have their place in the moral universe, it is clear that, under some circumstances, our rights and obligations are modified by the particular institutional contexts we find ourselves inhabiting, the specific roles we play within those contexts, the duties placed on us, and the unique privileges sometimes granted us to perform those duties.

The context-dependent nature of our obligations toward students has sometimes been recognized in moral and political philosophy. For example, Samantha Brennan and Robert Noggle have advanced the notion of role-dependent rights, the idea that our moral and political rights depend on the contexts in which we operate. Rights, they argue, "depend in part on the facts about the persons who bear them, facts about the relationship of which they are a part, facts about previous communities they have made, and facts about the societies in which they live."[1] They point out how professionals are given the ability to do certain things that others are not. Doctors can prescribe medications, for example, and lawyers can keep certain conversations confidential. For Brennan and Noggle, roles matter even for students: "One's role as a student confers certain rights against her teacher."[2] The justification of such rights is found in the need for social institutions to perform their prescribed roles. Without actors within those institutions who are given powers to act in particular ways, the institutions could not do what we ask them to do.

In this vein, the US Supreme Court has found that schools are specific spaces that modify and transform constitutional rights. In *Tinker v. Des*

Moines (1969), the court affirmed that students retain rights to speech and expression at school but, at the same time, stipulated that freedom of expression should be "applied in light of the special characteristics of the school environment," particularly the need to maintain order and discipline.[3] Since that time, the court has pointed to other characteristics of schools that seem relevant to the treatment of students. These include the importance of teaching students the norms of civic discourse (*Bethel School District No. 403 v. Fraser*, 1986), the need for a coherent curriculum (*Hazelwood School District v. Kuhlmeier*, 1988), and the importance of fighting illegal drug use (*Morse v. Frederick*, 2007).[4] In each case, the guidelines for the treatment of student speech grow out of considerations of the nature of the school environment. Constitutional rights, then, also depend on the context that one inhabits and the particular roles that one performs within that context. Schools, the courts have argued, are one context that transforms important individual rights.[5]

This makes sense. Schools are, without a doubt, social institutions with an important mission. But how should we conceptualize the social mission of schools? Here, it is necessary to ask about the goals that schools are trying to achieve and the sorts of roles and relationships that are vital to accomplishing these goals. The question is what makes schools *special*, different from other family, commercial, or government institutions. These special characteristics will largely define and construct a normative vision of school community. They will establish the goals of the moral community and, at the same time, set up the boundaries that community members must respect in pursuit of those goals. Moreover, the special characteristics will influence the sorts of relationships that should exist in schools, between educators and students, and therefore establish the forms of punishment and discipline that are appropriate. It is our contention that this idea of special characteristics should not only govern students' rights to speech, as the Supreme Court recognized, but also extend to issues of punishment and due process in schools. In what follows, we will look at the special characteristics that are central to discipline practices.[6]

The Special Characteristics of Schools

Special Characteristic 1: Educational Purposes   The first and perhaps most obvious characteristic of schools, the aspect that best defines their essence as moral communities, is that they are supposed to pursue educational goals. That is their raison d'être. The goals of American education can be divided into the vocational, the liberal, and the civic. The purely academic goals of schools—learning mathematics, science, history, languages, and so forth—are justified instrumentally, as means of accomplishing these larger goals. There is, we believe, some intrinsic value in knowing about academic subjects. The public interest in education, however, lies more in what this academic knowledge helps construct: citizens who are free and equal and can make positive contributions to the public good. Our focus, then, will be on the larger, social aims of schools and on the vocational, liberal, and civic goals of education. The nature of the moral community that educators should be building in schools will depend on the goals that the community is pursuing. If a particular notion of punishment is fundamentally incompatible with the vocational, liberal, and civic goals of education, then that notion of punishment should be rejected. The moral community of schools must be such that these goals can be accomplished.

The vocational goals consist in the preparation required for citizens to participate in the economy. At best, this involves thoughtfully exploring with students the vocational possibilities open to them and assisting students in choosing pathways that will be personally meaningful and contributory. Students will need to acquire a set of skills and dispositions that will guide them toward meaningful participation in the economy. While the public's focus is often on developing technical skills, particularly in math and science, employers are sometimes just as interested in the so-called "soft skills." These include communication, responsibility, teamwork, and social skills.[7] Other studies point to the desirability of abilities and characteristics such as ethics and problem-solving.[8]

The goal of liberal education is the development of autonomy and personal responsibility. Liberal educational goals grow out of the traditional political principles governing liberal-democratic societies—namely, liberty and equality. The idea behind the liberal goal of autonomy is that human beings should be given the opportunity to think for themselves and take personal responsibility for their beliefs and actions. Beyond the place of autonomy in the liberal political tradition, there are also independent moral arguments for its status as an educational goal. Autonomy is an important part of human happiness, since happiness would seem to increase as people become more able to choose their own lifestyles according to their preferences and values. Developing autonomy in education is also a critical part of how we as a society demonstrate respect for personhood. We show respect to human beings and their capacity to deliberate and make decisions when we encourage individuals to exercise this capacity and make fundamental decisions governing their own lives. Finally, autonomy is a necessary part of civic education—in order to overcome various forms of social manipulation and vote intelligently, individuals must use independent judgment and critical reason. From these moral arguments, it follows that children should be given the opportunity to develop the mental capacities and character traits associated with autonomy.

The development of autonomy is perhaps the most controversial goal of schooling. Autonomy has been advocated by a wide range of political thinkers, each advancing a particular vision of autonomy and how it is developed.[9] Autonomy as an educational aim is not without its critics, however, and some have argued that autonomy is harmful to democracy[10] or that it fails to recognize the importance of intellectual authority.[11] While we find the arguments for autonomy convincing, we are aware of its controversial status. The conception of punishment that we advance is not entirely dependent on acceptance of this goal; indeed, most of what we say will be relevant to those advocating only civic or vocational goals. We do believe, however, that recognizing the need for autonomy strengthens the case for the type of discipline and punishment we have in mind.

The last goal of education in democratic societies has to do with civic purposes. Education should help students live together peacefully and justly in a democratic society. At minimum, it seems that an adequate civic education provides for a basic historical, sociological, and governmental knowledge. It also encourages various dispositions that help people live together peacefully, such as tolerance, open-mindedness, forbearance of other viewpoints, respect for the rule of law, and the ability to engage with others under an umbrella of mutual respect in pursuit of justice. More broadly, any adequate notion of civic education would involve coming to know and care about how one's actions affect others. When disagreements arise, students should learn how talk with others as equals, resolving disputes in a cooperative and reciprocal way. The moral community of schools needs to be such that it encourages the development of these civic traits.

Special Characteristic 2: The Age of Students and Developmental Ethos Another important dimension of schools as moral communities is that they generally serve a population of minors, individuals who have not yet acquired the full set of legal and moral rights. These persons are usually denied full rights because we take their age as an indicator of immaturity. The very young usually have not developed the capacity or experience to make wise and informed decisions relating to their own present or future good. Many children in a candy store, for example, might make poor choices about what to eat because they do not know how to reason effectively about long-term consequences, because they lack knowledge of nutrition, or because they have not developed the strength of will to put long-term considerations in front of short-term pleasure.

On an abstract level, the youth of students forces us to recognize that schools, as moral communities, need to be places of growth and development. They are places where the governing assumption is precisely that students do *not* have fully refined judgment, rich experiences, advanced social skills, or deep knowledge of the consequences of their actions. This means that, more than other social institutions, schools need to be governed by what we could call a "developmental ethos." A developmental ethos highlights the importance of patience, allows for and even encourages mistakes, forgives, and emphasizes learning and progress over time. Schools must make decisions about how to correct students, obviously, but they must do so in ways that respect this developmental ethos. This means that punishments, when given, must be educational in nature rather than purely punitive, helping students to develop socially, emotionally, and civically. As we suggested in the first chapter, punishment allows for certain conversations to take place, which can serve educational or reformatory purposes. When punishment is understood purely as punitive retribution, it is incompatible with the developmental ethos. Retribution must assume moral responsibility, while schools must assume that responsibility is still in development.

Special Characteristic 3: School Association and Blurring Lines of Moral Responsibility   We often think of rights as individual rights. Citizens own themselves, and this self-ownership implies that citizens are fully responsible for their own actions. Theories of punishment often make assumptions about individual responsibility. Individual X made a free choice to hurt individual Y, so therefore X must be given a punishment proportionate to the harm caused to Y. But what if individual X did what was done because of social or biological forces beyond X's control? In that case, the socially determined nature of the action seems to undermine the argument for punishment. The focus, in those cases, should be on changing the social forces, not punishing the individuals.

Student misbehavior is sometimes accurately understood as the result of school failure, boring and mismanaged classrooms, or unskilled or underresourced teachers. Recall A. S. Neill's striking statement: "Thousands of teachers do their work splendidly without having to introduce fear of punishment. The others are incompetent misfits who ought to be driven out of the profession."[12] We would not put things nearly that strongly. Teachers often lack the resources and support that they need, and a turn to harsh punishment should not be surprising under such conditions. But Neill's point that bad schools are sometimes the cause of student misbehavior is surely correct. As Pedro Noguera states, "When we locate discipline problems exclusively in students and ignore the context in which problematic behavior occurs, we run the risk of overlooking some of the most important factors that give rise to the behavior."[13] The fact that schools are dealing with children and youth, who do not have full judgment, knowledge, and experience, also implies that the school itself is at least partly to blame for student behavioral issues and that it is therefore unfair to inflict burdens on students that are purely punitive in nature. A school as a moral community needs to be reflective—it needs to continually ask how it also bears moral responsibility for the behavior of students. No school is perfect, and the flaws of schools and teachers do translate into student behavioral problems.

Moreover, much of student action is, in fact, a cooperative effort between students and schools. The nature and degree of this entangled action make schools unique among social institutions. Schools provide a wide range of resources and forums for students and therefore supply avenues and platforms for student action. The actions of students and schools in these circumstances, and therefore the moral responsibility of students and schools, become intertwined and co-constructed. It becomes difficult to tell where the schools' moral responsibility ends and the students' moral responsibility begins.

Special Characteristic 4: Public Accountability and Legitimacy Most schools are either fully public institutions or private institutions that receive varying amounts of support from the public sector. Schools also have an important public charge—to prepare the next generation of citizens—and are therefore rightfully subject to different forms of public accountability and regulation. This matters in how we think about school relationships. For one thing, public accountability is related to the concept of legitimacy. Legitimacy, in fact, is the key feature of social institutions that justifies the exercise of state power. Governments can only justly enforce their laws through force when the government itself is legitimate. Compulsory schooling, then, can only be justly mandated by a government that is broadly seen as a legitimate expression of the public good. The same holds true for the use of force within schools—the just exercise of punishment within schools requires broad public legitimacy.

Legitimacy and trust in schools are also essential for both the health of the community and the proper functioning of the school as a social institution. This is particularly true for US schools at the local level. For example, US schools often rely on funding that comes from tax levies passed through referenda and on volunteers from the local community. These needs suggest that the mission of American schools cannot be accomplished without some degree of trust from local society. However we describe the moral nature of school community, then, it needs to include characteristics that allow schools to maintain legitimacy in the eyes of the public. School practices, if implemented in a discriminatory or arbitrary way, harm the trust that schools need within the communities they serve. They also harm the work of individual teachers, who rely on goodwill from parents and community members. Schools require public legitimacy, and misguided policies and practices can undermine the very legitimacy they depend on.

The Moral Community of Schools and Exclusionary Punishment

These special characteristics of schools help clarify the sorts of moral communities that schools should be and therefore the sort of punishment that is justified within them. Consider the aims and goals of schooling, which include the development of vocational soft skills, the promotion of autonomy, and the acquisition of civic dispositions of community engagement and understanding. We can begin to see that some disciplinary practices are antithetical to the educational aims of schooling. For example, while corporal punishment is problematic in ways that we have discussed earlier, many of the messages it sends also run counter to these educational aims: instead of fostering communication and dialogue, it prioritizes brute force. This seems incompatible with a civic education focused on cooperation and with the development of adults who can function in the workforce.

For now, let us focus for a moment on the much more widespread practices of suspension and expulsion. These also seem incompatible with educational goals, particularly when administered mechanically for minor offenses. These tactics are not educational because they require very little of students in terms of reflection and engagement—they do not help students to understand and take responsibility for their actions or to appreciate the nature of their social existence. Such sanctions do not offer the opportunity for "collective problem solving, learning, and growth."[14] There is little in the process of exclusion that helps students understand *why* what they did was wrong and that moves them toward more informed and autonomous action in the future. Students do not engage in the collective problem-solving or communication valued by employers, nor do they develop the empathy and responsiveness needed in democratic societies. Because the punishment involves little that is educational in nature, exclusionary practices fail to advance the liberal, civic, and vocational goals of education.

Exclusionary punishment also does little to take account of the other special characteristics of schools. First, with respect to a "developmental ethos," rather than fostering future growth, exclusionary practices have been shown to be highly damaging to students, limiting their future academic achievement and life prospects. Recall the conclusion of the American Academy of

Pediatrics, referenced earlier: "The adverse effects of out-of-school suspension and expulsion on the student can be profound."[15] Since there is so little opportunity to learn from exclusionary punishment, such practices ignore the fact that students are developing moral agents, in need of guidance and, often, forgiveness. Second, with respect to the school-associated nature of moral action, another special characteristic, exclusionary tactics fail to help educators identify practices that may be contributing to behavioral problems. Simply removing students from schools does not encourage schools to reflect on their own methods. Noguera describes why this reflection is so necessary, pointing to his observations of one school that attempted a form of exclusionary punishment: "When I spoke with teachers about the state of their classrooms now that the most disruptive students had been removed, the responses from the teachers were surprisingly similar. In nearly every case, I was told that while they appreciated the absence of the troublemakers, new students had emerged to take their place. Several teachers informed me that they were still experiencing disruptions in their classrooms, and some even suggested that the school needed one more teacher and one more isolated classroom to handle the remaining problem students."[16] With exclusion, there is no built-in moment of reflection that could have served these teachers, no recognition by the school of its own role in student behavior. Exclusion does little, then, to acknowledge that student behavior and school practices are intertwined. Third, with respect to public accountability and legitimacy, the last special characteristic of schools, the unequal application of disciplinary policies along racial and gender lines, particularly the unequal application of exclusionary punishment, seems to be doing lasting damage to the public's trust in schools. For oppressed groups, schools become agents of oppression. Claims implicating schools in the school-to-prison pipeline are a primary example of this threat to legitimacy. The messages of second-class citizenship that exclusionary practices can and do send are significantly damaging to schools' public standing among marginalized groups.

In sum, exclusionary punishment may inform students that the school authorities believe the students have done something wrong, but it does little to explain to them *why* their action was wrong. It asks very little of the students in terms of reflection and taking responsibility, and therefore does little to accomplish the educational purposes of schools. Students are left no better off when it comes to achieving the moral, civic, or vocational aims of education. Exclusionary punishment also does little to help educators reflect on their own practices, and it sows seeds of discontent among groups who are punished disproportionally in this way.

An Alternative: Restorative Justice

An alternative approach to school discipline has recently been advocated that seeks to improve this state of affairs: restorative justice. Restorative justice has been defined as "the process whereby parties with a stake in a specific offense collectively resolve to deal with the aftermath of an offense and its implications for the future."[17] This approach to conflict resolution and punishment is related to what one tends to find in various non-Western and premodern indigenous cultures, where small communities ask offenders to take responsibility and to repair the social wrong, seeking to reintegrate offenders into the community. The earliest applications of a restorative justice approach to social problems arose in the juvenile justice system, where there is much evidence of its positive outcomes.[18] Educators began adopting this approach in schools in the 1990s, with serious efforts beginning in the Australasian region.

Criminologist Howard Zehr, considered one of the pioneers of this approach in the criminal justice system, urges us to see "crime" as a breach of human relationships rather than as an abstract injury against the state.[19] The focus of restorative justice, for Zehr, is on how these harms can be healed and the community repaired. Rather than concentrating exclusively on "who is to blame," participants turn their attention toward "how can we solve this problem." The focus is on "conferences" rather than trials, conferences based in dialogue and the attainment of mutual understanding. In this view, the needs of the victims are primary—What do the victims need to feel safe and return to wholeness? The offender is asked to take responsibility and to assume an active role in repairing harm. This approach involves "truth telling" on the part of the victims, describing how they have been hurt. Dialogue is central, sometimes directly between the victim and the offender, and sometimes indirectly in cases of fear and power imbalances. The aim of the dialogue is to restore ties of community relationships.

In criminal justice, restorative justice conferences always involve the victim and the offender, and usually some sort of mediator. The mediator ensures that the conversation between the parties proceeds without fear and intimidation and that a dialogue among equals takes place. Usually, the victim explains what has happened, describing the impact that the offender's actions have had. The offender then responds, and a discussion ensues, often with powerful expressions of emotion. Lawrence Sherman and Heather Strang's research offers some details.[20] They reveal how the restorative dialogue often moves from vengefulness into empathy. This empathy is built among all participants in the dialogue: offenders better understand the hurt they have caused; victims better understand the context of the offender. Sherman and Strang contrast this move toward responsibility and empathy with how things transpire in typical legal proceedings, where offenders are encouraged to deny their involvement in the situation or minimize the harm that has been caused. Sherman and Strang describe how apologies are often present, but through the restorative encounter they are now transformed from mere words to real tokens of regret. This connects with the vision of punishment we endorsed in the first chapter, with the expressive function of punishment supplying a message that is "symbolically adequate" to what has occurred, opening up spaces for dialogical communication between all those affected.

While apologies alone are not always sufficient in the face of serious offense, they do have an extraordinary power to heal. Nicholas Tavuchis discusses how an apology is "doomed to fail" if it is supposed to resolve conflicts: "Why is this so? Very simply, because an apology, no matter how sincere or effective, does not and cannot undo what has been done. And yet, in a mysterious way and according to its own logic, this is precisely what it manages to do."[21] Canton builds on this question and speculates how apologies have such mysterious power:

> Perhaps part of the answer is that the past persists most significantly in the hearts, minds, and memories of those most affected by the incident. And memory is never a process of the mere retrieval of data, but an active matter of construction, reconstruction and interpretation, always influenced by concerns and interests of the present. The experience of the apology transforms the memory of the original offence, and an act for which apology has been given differs in precisely this respect from one where this has not taken place. Apology allows other memories to be laid down and subsequently drawn upon.[22]

A central goal of restorative justice is the restoration of dignity. Apology, in some cases, allows for the reconstruction or reinforcement of dignity. It is a recognition of the other, of the hurt caused to the other, and of one's responsibility in causing that hurt. Not just any apology, however, is sufficient. One can offer up an apology as mere words, an attempt to get out of responsibility, without understanding or acknowledging the harm that has been caused. An apology is not worthwhile unless the harm in question has been fully articulated and clarified. In restorative dialogue, the apology becomes more meaningful as the victim is able to directly describe to the offender the full impact of the harm that has been caused. The offender is in a context where listening is emphasized. Only after the victim feels that the offender has listened is an apology accepted.

Also, as we've seen, sometimes actions are required to show genuine remorse—some acceptance of shame or punishment that makes the apology meaningful. As part of restorative justice conferences, the parties reach an agreement about what is necessary for the "restoration" to take place. Sometimes, the agreement may include something like traditional punishment. The offenders may be asked to do certain things to show that they take their actions seriously and that they take responsibility for what they have done. Recall Duff's idea from the first chapter: a form of hard treatment may be a necessary expression of dismay (on the part of the victim and the community) and a pathway to showing genuine remorse (on the part of the offender). This sort of hard treatment can play a role in restorative justice. Such penance may include community service, detention, compensation, public apology, or even some form of shame or exclusion. But now after restorative discussions these punishments can come to be interpreted in new light—namely, as pathways to true apology and reintegration rather than punitive retribution. The punishment in a restorative context becomes a statement of meaning in an ongoing community conversation.

Along with dignity, another emphasis of restorative justice is the restoration of community ties. Focusing on blame and exclusion, we find that one of the chief problems with traditional approaches to punishment is how they serve to increase the distance of the offenders from communities. Punishment often stigmatizes offenders, making it difficult for them to live according to lawful standards and pushing them toward deviant identities and subcultures. The point of restorative justice is to try to reclaim the offender as part of a community. It does this by helping the offender know what to do to reenter regular human relationships.

Two additional aspects of restorative justice are particularly relevant to thinking about schools as moral communities. First is the issue of public confidence. There is some research indicating that restorative justice is supported by the general public. Studies gauging public attitudes toward restorative justice generally find that it is widely supported in the case of juvenile offenders (and for adult offenders too for less serious crimes).[23] There is also some research indicating that the restorative justice approach is supported by the general public in schools specifically. Valerie Braithwaite asked parents about their preferred views of school punishment, and summarizes her own findings in this way: "The model that meets with the most approval from parents is that which uses a restorative justice approach, while giving schools the capacity to move to retributive measures in the event that restorative strategies fail."[24] It seems likely, then, that using restorative justice, at least as a first response, would win support from parents and communities.

More generally, the view of many proponents of restorative justice is that restorative practices increase public confidence in social institutions. This occurs because in restorative justice models the process and outcome of the encounter have a better chance at winning the approval of *all* interested stakeholders. Restorative justice is seen as being more responsive to victims and communities and therefore as producing conclusions that are more likely to be seen as legitimate by all the involved parties. As Thom Brooks notes, "If the outcomes are good enough for those involved, then they should be good enough for the wider public."[25] Public confidence is particularly advanced when community members are included in the restorative conferencing. This inclusion makes sense from a restorative justice point of a view, because crime is never simply about offenders and victims but has ramifications for the larger society.

Second, restorative approaches often blur the line between victim and offender. Assignment of responsibility emerges from the dialogue and is not assumed at the beginning. According to Canton, "The roles of 'offender' and 'victim' are not necessarily pre-determined when the attempt at conflict resolution begins and indeed deciding who was in the wrong may matter less than achieving an outcome that sufficiently commands everyone's confidence."[26] This sort of openness about not only where responsibility lies but also what can be done moving forward is one of the strengths of the restorative justice approach. It allows for real dialogue and problem-solving. This makes sense in schools, where, as we have seen, lines of responsibility for student conduct are often blurry. Schools are better positioned to take some responsibility for student misbehavior—the dialogue of restorative justice can help educators pinpoint areas for improvement on the school side of things.

Admittedly, there are several limitations to the restorative justice approach. Some crimes might be too emotionally charged for any sort of dialogue to take place. Even many advocates of restorative justice argue that serious crimes, such as murder and rape, should not be approached through this paradigm. The depth of these types of harms would make a conference difficult, and perhaps retraumatizing for victims. There is also an issue with how restorative justice proceeds when there are steep power imbalances between victims and offenders. A good moderator may help balance some of the power imbalances, but differences in social background will likely still matter. Of course, power imbalances are present in all forms of punishment, not just in restorative justice approaches, so a critic of restorative conferences would have to show that the power imbalance in such conferences is more damaging than in other systems of punishment. Third, there is a problem of consistency in outcomes. In restorative justice, what matters is that all the stakeholders are satisfied. Some offenders may therefore "get off easy," while others may face stiff conditions in what they are asked to do. This may be a problem, to be sure, but Brooks points out that there is a type of *process consistency* within restorative justice—a consistent process is followed to address restorative needs.[27]

One might ask whether restorative justice should even be considered a paradigm of "punishment," or whether it is really just a way of solving problems. In one sense, restorative practices by themselves are not punishments for wrongdoing but are a process for determining a response to wrongdoing. Later on in the process, one outcome of a restorative dialogue might indeed be something resembling punishment—some sort of penance or burden or compensatory action may be agreed to. Or, the restorative practices might operate in tandem with a punishment administered through official channels. However, there is a sense in which a restorative dialogue is itself a form of punishment, if by punishment we mean a hardship imposed on an offender by a social authority because of the offense. A restorative conference might be imposed by the social authority (the school) because of such an offense. And while the dialogue might not be intended to be a hardship, per se, it is also certainly not something pleasant and might be perceived, subjectively, as a type of harsh treatment. In some cases, the difficult work of listening to a victim and expressing remorse might be all the hardship that is necessary.

Restorative justice has been implemented in some schools. Schools present a different context than juvenile justice systems, to be sure, and the educational purposes must be more of a priority in school settings than in the legal arena. The general idea of repairing relationships and restoring community through dialogue, however, is a goal that schools can endorse. A common practice in schools is the restorative "circle," where individuals within the school discuss their lives and work together to solve problems. The individuals in the circle cooperate to understand what has happened, who has been affected, and what can be done to restore relationships. Troi Bechet from the Center for Restorative Approaches argues that the goal of such practices is to work "with" students to solve problems, rather than to do things "to" them through traditional punishment: "This is about building an internal locus of control. Punishment is an external locus of control. If we want children to grow up to be socially responsible adults, we need them to believe that they should do the right thing because it is the right thing to do."[28] Restorative justice asks students to do real moral work.

The Moral Community of Schools and Restorative Justice

In developing this internal locus of control, restorative justice seems to strongly align with the moral community of schools. This hints at the argument we would now like to make explicit: a restorative approach is justified in schools because it best matches the aims and values that should undergird the American school system. A restorative justice approach, in other words, coheres with the educational mission of schools and the other special characteristics of the school environment. Indeed, we would go further: restorative approaches are required in schools as a matter of justice, given the types of social institutions that schools are and the purposes that are assigned to them. This approach to punishment best matches the idea of schools as moral communities, properly understood.

Educational Goals and Restorative Justice   The first thing to point out is that restorative practices and the rich dialogues they involve are themselves deeply educational. They are a way to not simply discipline but also teach. Through such practices, students learn about human relationships and about themselves as responsible moral agents. Such practices ask students to think about who they are and about how they should be interacting with others. An important part of civic education is to help students know how to understand and work with others as equals in a shared way of life. Students need to comprehend how their actions affect others. Students need to develop skills of empathy, to put themselves in the positions of others and imagine how they might feel. Rather than just removing students from classrooms, restorative circles engender discussions that move students toward these educational goals, and they do so in perhaps the most relevant way imaginable: the students are solving real social problems with their peers and teachers. Building social knowledge, building empathy, and building pathways to cooperation and reconciliation in community are the explicit goals of restorative conferences. And while it is perhaps most natural to frame the educational nature of restorative dialogue in terms of civic education, it is easy to see that such experiences will also help students develop the soft skills that will serve them in the workforce. After all, vocational contexts also demand conflict resolution, communication, and relationship mending.

Consider also the goal of building autonomy and responsibility in students, one of the key aspects of a liberal education. A liberal education strives to help students see themselves as actors who can make responsible choices for themselves about how to live. It involves telling one's story, admitting mistakes, and taking responsibility for those mistakes in order to make things right. These activities are all a part of restorative justice conferences—they help students to develop that "internal locus of control," to see themselves as the authors of their own lives, as people who have the strength of will to make their own decisions. Students also see themselves as responsible for and capable of repairing relationships that they might damage. They are given a voice in the circle and are able to explain their experiences and emotions. In so doing, they learn that their voice matters and their actions can shape the world. Little of this happens as part of other disciplinary practices, but it is central to restorative justice.

The Developmental Ethos and Restorative Justice   The school is an environment that needs to recognize that children are still learning and developing rather than entering it as finished moral beings. The school needs to be a place where mistakes can be made and where errors do not become life sentences. Zero tolerance policies, particularly when paired with exclusionary discipline, seem to forget this basic characteristic of schools as moral communities. Restorative justice sees both students and schools as developing together, continually in process. Under restorative justice, questions about moral responsibility and blame (a problematic concept when dealing with children) are not the singular focus—learning together and collective problem-solving are also part of the process. The practices themselves become educational rather than (simply) punitive. At their best, other forms of punishment—exclusion, shame, corporal punishment—signal that an action is wrong, but they do not help convey *why* an action is wrong. Under restorative justice, schools become places of apology, forgiveness, and restoration. Therefore, they better respect the developmental ethos.

The School-Associated Nature of Action and Restorative Justice   As pointed out earlier, in many forms of restorative justice, the categories of "offender" and "victim" are softened and the restorative dialogue is allowed to uncover multiple lines of responsibility. This is particularly important in school settings, because students and educators bear joint responsibility for much of what occurs there. There is no doubt that schools can contribute to student behavior. Where the school is implicated, the truth telling should come from all sides. It should come from the educators involved, jointly exploring with students how they can do better as teachers, and from the students, exploring how their actions can better show respect for others. As Tom Macready has observed, restorative justice approaches allow teachers and administrators a chance to better learn how to meet the needs of the students.[29] In fact, some research has indicated that teachers participating in a pilot project of restorative practices were more willing to reflect on their relationships and interactions with students.[30] This assumption of joint responsibility should be a key factor governing restorative conferences in schools. Such conferences open up opportunities for reflection, allowing educators to assume at least partial responsibility for what has happened. There is, in fact, unique potential in restorative justice to honor this special characteristic of the school.

Public Legitimacy and Restorative Justice   As we have seen, an important concern for proponents of restorative justice is building public trust and confidence. We have seen some studies indicate public support for restorative justice in schools and for its use with young juvenile offenders. Support is particularly strong for using restorative justice as a first option and for minor offenses. This implies a potential for restorative practices to achieve public backing and maintain or increase legitimacy. It is sometimes the case that communities lose confidence in schools because of schools' disciplinary practices. This is particularly true in the case of marginalized students and their families. If such families perceive that punishment is given in a capricious or arbitrary way or, worse, given in a way that is fundamentally hostile or discriminatory, a crisis of legitimacy is a possible result. Restorative justice seeks to revive community confidence in the disciplinary practices of schools. It does this by seeking a resolution that is acceptable to all interested stakeholders. Greater community confidence can be more effectively accomplished by having trusted representatives from the community engage in restorative conferences in schools—this representation is particularly helpful if there are differences in background between staff and students (for example, if the school has a mostly White teaching staff and a mostly Black student body). Such a representative can facilitate the process of truth telling if that person commands wide respect. Practiced in this way, restorative justice helps schools regain the trust and legitimacy they may have lost.

Overall, then, when it comes to the educational goals of schools, the youth of students, the fact of school-associated action, and the school's need for public trust and legitimacy, restorative practices better respect school environments and the moral community that should exist there. They are a more suitable match for schools than exclusionary punishment and corporal punishment. Punishment has, we have argued, an expressive function that gives voice to community disapproval. But the specific type of punishment can add layers of meaning on top of this generic expression of disapproval. We have called these additional meanings the "secondary expressions" of punishment. As part of its secondary expression, exclusionary punishment seems to send the message that a student's presence is not wanted or valued and that the school believes it would be better off if the student were not around. Corporal punishment sends a message about the acceptability of physical violence and that "might makes right." Restorative justice sends more productive messages. While acknowledging problems and harms and asking for responsibility, restorative practices also reaffirm the importance of voice, allow for dialogue, indicate mutual respect, ask for reflection, and establish appropriate norms of human interaction. Through these secondary expressions, restorative justice becomes the most educational way of engaging with student behavior.

For these reasons, the moral community of schools should be built around an overarching framework of restorative justice. At the same time, it will be useful to blend this framework with some of the best insights from the retributive tradition. Some disciplinary problems in schools (like most cases of tardiness, for example) do not involve moral issues—they simply present practical challenges to resolve. In such cases, restorative circles can take on an atmosphere of joint problem-solving rather than moral judgment. The open communication will be enough to resolve the issue. There are times, however, when the school community has been harmed in significant ways and some form of restoration and reconciliation will need to occur. In such cases, the resources of retributive justice—some sort of burden and blame, carefully considered—are appropriate. Sometimes, the burden that is agreed to through restorative discussion will look very much like traditional punishment. These punishments can be important vehicles for community restoration. Recall from chapter 1 how the burden of punishment can be an instrument for legitimate public censure—communicating the seriousness of certain actions to the larger school community. Recall also that when a burden is accepted by an offender, it can facilitate the process of apology and reconciliation. The punitive burden can enact what Bennett calls the "apology ritual," and the community can be restored. For this to happen, though, the preexisting school relationships need to be positive so that students care about reintegration—if students lack connection to the community, it is doubtful they will want to restore it. Also required is that the punishment be symbolically adequate, or as Bennett says, that it asks offenders "to undertake the sort of reparative action that they would be motivated to undertake were they genuinely sorry for what they have done."[31] If a student is asked to clean up after an act of vandalism, that is a punishment that connects to the misdeed and, when it is accepted by the offender, allows for a feeling of reparation, of making right. Restorative discussions can help collectively determine what might be an adequate punitive response for a student who harmed another. While restorative justice practices should undergird the process of reconciliation in schools, then, certain elements associated with retribution might also be necessary for such reconciliation to be achieved.

Criticism of Restorative Justice in Schools

Not everyone is convinced by the need for this approach. Critics of restorative justice in education—and sometimes even educators themselves—complain that restorative practices make it difficult for teachers to maintain order in the classroom. Students, released from the threat of punishment, are now free to bully their peers and their teachers, misbehave, and disrupt classrooms. One critic, Paul Sperry, ridicules the ideas that schools should "respect students," that school problems may be the result of racial misunderstanding, and that ineffective teaching may be a part of the discipline problems schools face.[32] Not all critics are as dismissive of the underlying ethical concerns of restorative justice, but worries persist that student behavior will worsen without traditional punishments.[33] These critics might claim, in our language, that achieving the educational goals of schooling requires a safe and stable learning environment, that this should also be one of the special characteristics of schools, and that restorative practices work against this requirement. This is an important point, and the critics are correct: a safe and ordered environment is essential to a functioning school context. It might be better for the offending student not to be expelled, but is it better for everyone else?

In response, we would like to highlight a few points about restorative justice as practiced in schools. First, the existing research on restorative justice does not support the idea that schools become more chaotic under restorative practices. Early research in this area did not conduct direct causal testing of restorative justice interventions. The early studies lacked the sort of randomization and control group that would allow for causal claims to be made. This research often included simple reports from observers or pre- and post-intervention comparisons without control groups. Still, in a review of this literature up to 2016, Trevor Fronius and his coauthors summarized a body of research indicating that restorative justice approaches generally tended to have the following effects. Such approaches

> improved "school climate,"
> increased "student connectedness" and community engagement,
> decreased "disciplinary disparities, fighting, bullying, and suspensions,"
> decreased the number of reoffending students, and
> decreased student absenteeism.

The review also indicates fairly mixed results related to gains in academic achievement. Some studies found a slight gain in students' grade point averages and graduation rates after the implementation of restorative programs, while other studies reported no significant change in grade point average. The report continually highlights the limitations of the available data, with the authors concluding, "In general, the research evidence to support RJ [restorative justice] in schools is still in a nascent state. Despite the exponential growth of RJ in U.S. schools, and some evidence of its effectiveness abroad, the evidence to date is limited and the research that has been published lacks the internal validity necessary to exclusively attribute outcomes to RJ. However, the preliminary evidence does suggest that RJ may have positive effects across several outcomes related to discipline, attendance and graduation, climate and culture, and various academic outcomes."[34]

Two more recent and well-designed studies from the RAND Corporation found a complex and sometimes conflicting mixture of results.[35] School climate seemed to improve and suspension rates were lower under restorative policies, but classroom climates were sometimes reported to be worse and academic achievement suffered, at least in schools with predominantly Black students. Critics of restorative justice have pointed to these findings as evidence that restorative justice is simply unworkable. As RAND commentators note, however, the dip in achievement seemed to occur in schools that did *not* reduce suspensions, suggesting that "it had more to do with the difficulty teachers had in meeting all the demands on their time than with disruption by students who otherwise would have been suspended."[36] They also note that implementation was highly variable across schools and teachers. Overall, they point out that the two studies, together, indicate that students *who actually experienced restorative practices* reported less bullying, greater connection to peers, and better classroom climates. The two studies do not support the idea that restorative practices make schools more chaotic and unruly.

Second, we note that the real worth of the literature is not in helping us see whether restorative justice "works" overall—restorative justice is really a cluster of different practices and strategies, not a stable "intervention" that can be tested like a new drug treatment.[37] At this point, the restorative justice approach offers a wide range of possibilities and strategies that can be tested, and only a small number have actually been researched. Success or failure of one restorative strategy in one context does little to speak to the overall effectiveness of the paradigm. The best studies help us see which practices might be useful, under which conditions, for which group of students. Not all implementations would or should be the same across all contexts. Given the ethical necessity of restorative justice and the ethical failure of alternative methods, at this point initial difficulties are simply an indication to try something else. The first challenge is to find out which restorative practices work best given the scope of contextual factors, and only then can this type of approach be evaluated against other approaches.

Third, the literature has noted that restorative justice requires significant time, resources, and cultural change.[38] It seems clear that teachers, under restorative policies, often feel unsupported or that they lack the tools to deal with difficult behavioral problems. It goes without saying that teachers and administrators require applied training and ongoing mentorship in this form of classroom management, which some districts struggle to provide.[39] This is a challenge that deserves further exploration, to be sure, but it does not seem like an insurmountable problem. The disenchantment that some teachers feel with restorative practices is understandable—such practices do take time and energy. Educators' reservations about restorative justice point to a larger truth about school discipline. We have seen in the past that educators who faced potentially chaotic environments (such as one-room schoolhouses or overcrowded charity schools) and lacked training and resources reached for whatever tools promised to help maintain control of their environments—historically, those tools could be quite brutal. From this, we should learn that the ethics of punishment will not survive first contact with a teaching reality that is underresourced and neglected. Part of what allows schools to be proper moral communities is the support from the larger community. If class sizes balloon, if quality professional training is unavailable, and if mental health and counseling services are lacking, the school community will suffer, and questionable disciplinary practices will be the inevitable consequence as teachers strive to maintain control. If we are to ask teachers to play the proper educational role with respect to discipline, we must give them the resources to make that possible.

Restorative justice assumes an optimistic and demanding view of schooling but not a completely unrealistic or overly idealized view. It is unlikely that widespread adoption of restorative justice can occur until the resource supports are in place and entire schools and districts substantially shift their thinking. We are encouraged by schools that have overcome these boundaries and have moved toward adopting this new approach—see, for example, the Oakland Unified School District, which saw reduced suspensions, reductions in the Black-White discipline gap, and improved academic performance, among several other positive indicators, after implementing restorative justice approaches in 2005.[40] These examples serve as a proof of concept, demonstrating that schools, under the right conditions, can put this approach into practice.

So, how should we think about restorative approaches under nonideal conditions, when resources are scarce? In such circumstances, there are still opportunities to learn from the spirit of restorative justice, using microtactics to move in modest ways toward the ideal. At the level of individual teachers, these tactics would involve building better relationships and increasing the level of moral dialogue with students, focusing on understanding and solving behavioral problems rather than quickly imposing traditional punishments.

Under nonideal circumstances, teachers might also consider limiting the scope of restorative justice and implementing hybrid approaches. For example, for minor infractions (gum chewing and tardiness) and one-off instances of disruptive behavior, rather than invoking a full restorative circle, educators can employ traditional classroom-management strategies. For ongoing or morally problematic behavior, a richer moral conversation might then be justified. If traditional punishments are deemed necessary, a hybrid approach might involve restorative conferencing concurrent with a traditional punishment. These hybrid approaches might capture some of the ethical spirit of restorative justice, while acknowledging practical limitations.

Conclusion

Restorative justice practices best match the special characteristics of schools. By respecting elements of schools understood as moral communities, restorative practices avoid the heavy-handed moralism of earlier education systems and the damaging managerialism of contemporary methods. In contrast to exclusionary punishment, they infuse schools with a rich dialogue about moral responsibility, about the effects of our actions on others, and about how broken relationships can be repaired. They are disciplinary practices that are themselves educational. At the same time, it is also important to remember that traditional punishment practices, particularly suspension and expulsion, often have devastating consequences for those students most in need of support. These are not acceptable alternatives to restorative justice. Traditional punishments fail to address the core reasons for student misbehavior.

The strength of having restorative dialogues with students is that, when done properly, such conversations give educators access to perspectives that will help them improve their practice. Through listening to students in restorative dialogue, reflective educators can self-correct the problems of teaching practice in a way that makes these methods uniquely attractive and uniquely necessary. Such practices build the sort of moral community required in institutions dedicated to education. The moral case for restorative justice, then, is compelling. There is an argument for "sticking with" restorative justice as the overriding paradigm for school discipline, finding ways to ensure that it works for all students and teachers, and not giving up at the first negative study of or sign of difficulty at its implementation. Restorative justice, or something like it, is what the moral community of schools requires.

Punishment, Properly Conceived

School punishment is broken. As we have argued repeatedly throughout this book, punishment falls inequitably on different groups of children, with boys, children of color (including girls), and students with disabilities bearing the brunt. In some areas of the country, children are still swatted with planks of wood, sometimes sustaining lasting physical and emotional injuries. Almost everywhere children are suspended from school for minor, discretionary offenses, reducing their opportunities to learn, lowering their attachment to the school community, and increasing their chances of court involvement. The risk of court involvement has even risen *within* schools as uniformed school resource officers, or SROs, patrol the hallways and respond to classroom disorder with handcuffs and arrests. What public good could these forms of correction possibly achieve?

Many Americans respond to this question with vague references to order, safety, deterrence, or character formation as the primary purposes of education, usually with the assumption that schools today are laxer and unrulier than they used to be. These claims do not stand up to scrutiny. As we have demonstrated, schools have always confronted disruptive students, whom they have tried to control through a mixture of brute force, public shame, emotional appeals, and spatial segregation. Such methods, drawn from irreconcilable philosophies and oriented toward poorly defined goals, have not only been prone to abuse but also impeded serious consideration of the purpose of punishment. Lacking a clear sense of what harsh treatment is supposed to accomplish (or how) puts its effectiveness beyond the reach of empirical evidence. Current arrangements serve some interests, surely, but they are hardly those of schoolchildren or the public as a whole. The current regime of corporal and exclusionary punishment most directly benefits principals and teachers, whose professional status has long depended on the ability to preserve traditional standards of authority and academic progress in the classroom. The rise of bureaucracy and professionalization during the twentieth century stressed teachers' expertise in classroom management, but the underlying dynamics of modern disciplinary tactics remain much the same as in early eras: it is easier to punish disruptive students than to engage them. More broadly, the existing regime of school punishment benefits those unwilling to adequately fund public education, those with a vested interest in White supremacy, and those advocating even earlier criminalization and control of impoverished youth.

It may seem strange, given all of these shortcomings, that we ultimately endorse punishment in schools. We should specify, of course, that we mean punishment *properly conceived*, and that our vision bears little resemblance to the sorts of inflexible, inequitable, and incoherent systems at work in so many schools in the United States.

In our view, punishment is a fundamentally *moral* undertaking and thus an antidote to merely procedural or bureaucratic penalties. One of the defining features of punishment is its expressive function. Punishment should express the voice of the public on issues of moral concern. It should send a message, perhaps to the larger school community, but certainly to a student who has done something wrong. Punishment is necessary because sometimes words of explanation are themselves not adequate, symbolically, to capture the importance of what has occurred. Not all actions of concern to a community are moral problems, to be sure. When issues of efficiency or social coordination are at stake, penalties and sanctions can be employed without the sense of moral disapproval that comes with punishment. Too often, however, schools lose the distinction between the moral and the conventional. If moral concerns are indeed at stake, this is a time to bring the resources of punishment and the expressive function to bear.

We also see punishment, when properly conceived, as unavoidably *educative*. The moral community of schools is necessarily built around educational concerns. The purpose of the expressive function in schools is to provide a framework for moral education and the civic, liberal, and even vocational purposes associated with it. Punishment can be anti-educational in many ways, alienating students from the school community, giving educators cover for inadequate classroom environments, shuttling students into the criminal justice system, or simply making no demands that students engage in moral deliberation and reflection, resulting in little lasting change or moral development. Sometimes the "secondary expressions" of certain forms of punishment—such as corporal punishment and exclusion—send unproductive messages to students. To be meaningfully educational, the hard treatment of punishment needs a robust, discursive context: explanations, descriptions of harm, reason giving, apologies, and reconciliations. Punishment is justified in education because it has the power, when carefully used, to make certain educational conversations possible. The recent turn toward restorative justice in schools holds the potential to facilitate these sorts of conversations, we argue, thereby making punishment educational and constructing the sort of moral community that schools ought to be.

In its primary and secondary expressions, punishment is *communal*. The community and the individual cannot be fully separated. Student behavior is at least partly dependent on how schools are structured, how teaching is undertaken, and how classroom life is organized. It is also dependent on how students feel in hallways and classrooms—whether they feel they are cared for, listened to, respected, and valued. Schools, as we have noted, should always be attentive to how they contribute to student misbehavior. Schools will need to look inward at their own beliefs, policies, and cultures, just as they ask students to look inward. At the same time, schools do not exist apart from their larger communities. If our neighborhoods, cities, and states neglect schools, letting them crumble and deteriorate, or disparage teachers, schools will lack the resources to undertake their disciplinary and educational missions. And if outside institutions—such as law enforcement—do not embody moral values and civic respect, they can hardly ask schools to successfully enforce these norms in children. Although the phrase "it takes a village to raise a child" has become something of a platitude, it is important to stress that when it comes to moral education in public schools, community bonds, reciprocity, and public vigilance remain paramount.

Punishment must be grounded not merely in the bounds of law or tradition but also in the precepts of *justice*. In deciding how to respond to student misbehavior, schools must ensure that consequences are proportional to transgressions, that children have the ability to control their actions and the moral understanding necessary for culpability and blame, and, most of all, that procedures for discipline are applied predictably and impartially, without targeting students for their race, gender, background, culture, or appearance. School punishment plays out against a larger background of social inequality, and it would be naive to ignore the ways that students experience injustice both outside of school and within it. Thus, teachers and administrators must be especially sensitive to students' and families' perceptions of fairness, as well as to their own, when condemning student behavior. Schools must earn the legitimacy that makes punishment consensual and authoritative.

We mentioned in the beginning that a consideration of school punishment helps us think about education more broadly. It opens up the opportunity to rethink assumptions about the role of teachers, the responsibilities of students, the nature of schools as institutions, and the purposes of education. Reflecting on punishment, we have seen, pushes us to think with renewed clarity about the purposes of schools and about the fundamental goals educators are pursuing. It asks that we stipulate the sorts of communities that schools need to be, and that we envision the sorts of relationships that should exist between teachers and students, given the duties and responsibilities we assign to educational institutions. Part of what we have described, historically and in terms of the special characteristics of schools, goes beyond punishment, addressing different facets of life within schools. Thinking about punishment asks us to rethink the role of students: children who are not yet full moral agents, ready to assume responsibility for their behaviors and actions, but whom the school wants to make so. This goal suggests that schools need to ask more from their students—to reflect, to explain, to engage, to apologize, to problem solve—not only in punishment situations but in other contexts as well. Students are not passive recipients of the actions of teachers and administrators, in either pedagogy or punishment. Punishment, then, also asks us to reexamine the role of educators. Educators are given the authority to punish, to utilize its expressive function, for the purpose of initiating students into a moral life. With this authority come responsibilities that are both inspiring and demanding. Educators are not simply subject-matter experts or pedagogical specialists; rather, they are mentors to youth and children, guides to the moral lives of their communities. To think about punishment, in the end, is to think about relationships, and this touches on every corner of the school building.

Acknowledgments

We wish to thank Randall Curren and Jonathan Zimmerman, who brought us together, started our thinking, and encouraged us along the way. They have provided excellent feedback and support throughout this process. Elizabeth Branch Dyson was both insightful critic and enthusiastic cheerleader for this project, and two anonymous readers from the University of Chicago Press provided detailed and constructive guidance that greatly improved this book. We thank Winston Thompson, John Tillson, and all the participants in the Pedagogies of Punishment workshop: Abigail J. Beneke, J. C. Blokhuis, Helen Brown Coverdale, Randall Curren, Michael Hand, George W. Holden, Lily Lamboy, Garry S. Mitchell, Laura Oxley, and Ashley Taylor. It was a pleasure to exchange ideas with this talented and formidable group. We also thank colleagues and students for the many informal exchanges, too numerous to mention but too valuable to ignore. We would also like to thank our families for the joy and love that make all other things possible. Finally, we thank the publishers of *Theory and Research in Education* for giving us permission to republish Bryan R. Warnick and Campbell F. Scribner, "Discipline, Punishment, and the Moral Community of Schools," *Theory and Research in Education* 18, no. 1 (2020): 98–116.

Notes

Introduction

1. "Student's 'Unfair Punishment' Sparks Changes for School Discipline," WSB-TV Atlanta, May 11, 2015, https://www.wsbtv.com/news/local/students-unfair-punishment-sparks-changes-school-d/53873930/.

2. Meek, "School Discipline 'As Part of the Teaching Process,'" 171–72; S.G. ex rel. A.G. v. Sayreville Bd. of Education, 333 F.3d 417, 418 (3d Cir. 2003).

3. Betsy Hammond, "Southern Oregon Elementary School Will Change Harsh Consequences for Tardiness after Facebook Post Prompts Widespread Complaints," *The Oregonian*, January 9, 2019, https://www.oregonlive.com/education/2015/02/southern_oregon_elementary_sch.html.

4. Kyra Gurney, "In Miami, Disruptive Students Are Handcuffed, Undergo Psych Exams," *Education Week*, February 2, 2018.

5. Morris, *Pushout*, chapter 2.

6. Debbie Truong, "Parents Sue Fairfax Schools, Alleging Improper Seclusion and Restraint of Students with Disabilities," *Washington Post*, October 8, 2019, https://www.washingtonpost.com/local/education/parents-sue-fairfax-schools-allege-improper-seclusion-and-restraint-of-students-with-disabilities/2019/10/08/066166dc-e9f8-11e9-85c0-85a098e47b37_story.html; Jennifer Smith Richards, Jodi S. Cohen, and Lakeidra Chavis, "The Quiet Rooms," Pro Publica, November 19, 2019, https://features.propublica.org/illinois-seclusion-rooms/school-students-put-in-isolated-timeouts/.

7. "Disturbing Bodycam Footage Shows 10-Year-Old with Autism Being Pinned," *Daily Mail*, August 13, 2018, https://www.dailymail.co.uk/news/article-6056693/Bodycam-footage-shows-10-year-old-boy-autism-handcuffed-school-resource-officer.html; Scott v. County of San Bernardino, 903 F.3d 943 (2018).

8. Henrietta Cook, "The Push to Ban 'Unfair' Group Punishment in Schools," *The Age*, July 10, 2019, https://www.theage.com.au/national/victoria/the-push-to-ban-unfair-group-punishment-in-schools-20190710-p525xk.html.

9. This data is from 2011–2012. See Gershoff, Purtell, and Holas, *Corporal Punishment in U.S. Public Schools*, 6.

10. Moriah Balingit, "Racial Disparities in School Discipline Are Growing, Federal Data Show," *Washington Post*, April 24, 2018, https://www.washingtonpost.com/local/education/racial

-disparities-in-school-discipline-are-growing-federal-data-shows/2018/04/24/67b5d2b8-47e4
-11e8-827e-190efaf1f1ee_story.html.

11. United States Government Accountability Office, *Discipline Disparities for Black Students, Boys, and Students with Disabilities.*

12. For a recent example of this genre of criticism, see Hess and Eden, "When School-Discipline 'Reform' Makes Schools Less Safe."

13. Garland, *Punishment and Modern Society*, 9.

14. Canton, *Why Punish?*, 27.

Chapter One

1. The "received view" is presented and criticized in McPherson, "Punishment: Definition and Justification." It is still the most widely accepted philosophical definition of punishment. McPherson is summarizing the famous views of Antony Flew, S. I. Benn, and H. L. A. Hart. See Flew, "The Justification of Punishment"; Benn, "An Approach to the Problems of Punishment"; and Hart, "The Presidential Address." A discussion of this definition in the context of education can be found in Peters, *Ethics and Education.*

2. For a discussion, see Boonin, *The Problem of Punishment.*

3. Hanna, "Say What? A Critique of Expressive Retributivism," 124.

4. This is the position taken by Nel Noddings in *Happiness and Education.*

5. This focus on punishment as only applicable to violation of the law can be found in Brooks, *Punishment.*

6. For examples of this position, see Feinberg, "The Expressive Function of Punishment"; von Hirsch, *Censure and Sanctions*; Duff, *Punishment, Communication, and Community*; and Wringe, *An Expressive Theory of Punishment.*

7. Feinberg, "The Expressive Function of Punishment," 397–98.

8. See Goodman, "Is Punishment Passé?"

9. See Feinberg, "The Expressive Function of Punishment."

10. Goodman, "School Discipline in Moral Disarray."

11. In the case of cross-racial interpretations, these judgments can often go badly awry. White teachers often misinterpret the intentions and moral agency of Black students. See Lamboy, Taylor, and Thompson, "Paternalistic Aims and (Mis)Attributions of Agency."

12. Goodman, "School Discipline in Moral Disarray," 218–19.

13. Bennett, *The Apology Ritual*, 8.

14. Wringe, *An Expressive Theory of Punishment.*

15. Peters, *Ethics and Education*, 275.

16. Duff, *Punishment, Communication, and Community*, 95.

17. Duff acknowledges that current prison systems in most countries are not structured to promote remorse or reflection. In this sense, while he endorses the idea of punishment, he strongly criticizes penal institutions as currently constituted. Prisons, he says, should be structured to treat prisoners "as citizens, not as outcasts." See Duff, *Punishment, Communication, and Community*, 150.

18. Wringe, *An Expressive Theory of Punishment*, 66–87.

19. Brooks, *Punishment*, 106–11.

20. Pieper and Pieper, *Smart Love*, 208.

21. Classical sources for debate include Immanuel Kant, for the retributivist view, and J. S. Mill, for the utilitarian, future-consequences view. See Kant, "Justice and Punishment"; and

Mill, *The Collected Works of John Stuart Mill*, XXVIII: 266–72. For examples of the contemporary debate, see the conflicting essays by H. J. McCloskey and T. L. S. Sprigge in *Philosophical Perspectives on Punishment*, ed. Gertrude Ezorsky.

22. This is the view of Hart, *Punishment and Responsibility*.

23. National Research Council Committee on Deterrence and the Death Penalty, *Deterrence and the Death Penalty*.

24. Duff, *Punishment, Communication, and Community*, 91. Note that Duff himself is not a proponent of punishment for moral education, although he holds a somewhat related view. He objects to moral education as being a justification for punishment, because of the following: (1) It is unclear that the problem with moral offenders is that they need more education. Often offenders know what they are doing is wrong and, as moral agents, choose a path. (2) It is unclear whether punishment is the best method for moral education, even if it is a possible method— why not a sermon? Duff, however, seems to be operating under a truncated notion of education. He himself endorses punishment as an act of persuasion to help people care more about the moral dimensions of what they have done. Persuasion for inner reform in this way is clearly an educational project, if anything is.

25. The idea that schools should be neutral with respect to competing moral positions was perhaps best exemplified by the "value clarification" movement of the 1960s and 1970s. This approach to moral education asked students to explore their own moral beliefs and encouraged teachers to remain neutral or nonjudgmental. The foundational text is Simon, Howe, and Kirschenbaum, *Values Clarification*. While few educators endorse this position today, the idea that schools should be neutral with respect to different views of morality remains common.

26. See, for example, Kohn, *Unconditional Parenting*, 70.

27. A classic source is Skinner, *Beyond Freedom and Dignity*. A 2002 meta-analysis supported some of these claims with respect to corporal punishment. Corporal punishment often (but not always) increased children's immediate compliance, but no more so than other disciplining methods. At the same time, it was found that corporal punishment decreased internalization of moral principles and attitudes: "Consistent with previous research that power assertion impedes children's moral internalization . . . the studies examined here found corporal punishment to be associated overall with decreases in children's moral internalization, operationalized as their long-term compliance, their feelings of guilt following misbehavior, and their tendencies to make reparations upon harming others." Gershoff, "Corporal Punishment by Parents and Associated Child Behaviors and Experiences," 550. For an updated look at the literature, see Gershoff, "More Harm Than Good."

28. Neill, *Summerhill*, 124.

29. Peters, *Ethics and Education*, 279.

30. For an extended discussion, see Kohn, *Beyond Discipline*.

31. Kohn, *Unconditional Parenting*, 70.

32. Bailey, *From Front Porch to Back Seat*.

33. See Gershoff, "More Harm Than Good," 35–40.

34. This particular number comes from Crenshaw, Nanda, and Ocen, *Black Girls Matter*, 16–17.

35. United States Government Accountability Office, *Discipline Disparities for Black Students, Boys, and Students with Disabilities*, 12–15, 3.

36. de Brey et al., *Status and Trends in the Education of Racial and Ethnic Groups*, 96–97.

37. Council on School Health, "Out-of-School Suspension and Expulsion," e1001–e1002.

38. Lacoe and Steinberg, "Do Suspensions Affect Student Outcomes?," 57.

39. Gregory, Skiba, and Noguera, "The Achievement Gap and the Discipline Gap," 60.

40. Morris and Perry, "The Punishment Gap."

41. de Brey et al., *Status and Trends in the Education of Racial and Ethnic Groups*, 97.

42. Peter Moore, "Poll Results: Punishment," YouGov, September 17, 2014, https://today.you gov.com/topics/politics/articles-reports/2014/09/17/poll-results-punishment.

43. Gershoff and Font, "Corporal Punishment in U.S. Public Schools," 3.

44. Human Rights Watch/ACLU, *Impairing Education*.

45. Gershoff and Font, "Corporal Punishment in U.S. Public Schools," 7–8. Boys and students with disabilities were also much more likely to be punished.

46. The number 4,000 comes from the Education Week Research Center. Sarah D. Sparks and Alex Harwin, "Corporal Punishment Use Found in Schools in 21 States," *Education Week*, August 23, 2016, https://www.edweek.org/ew/articles/2016/08/23/corporal-punishment-use-found -in-schools-in.html; Gershoff and Font, "Corporal Punishment in U.S. Public Schools," 1.

Chapter Two

1. MacLeod, *The Age of the Child*, 1–3.

2. Recalling his schooling in fourth-century Rome, Saint Augustine laments that "parents scoffed at the torments which we boys suffered at the hands of our masters." Augustine, *The Confessions*, I.9.14.

3. Bailyn, *Education in the Forming of American Society*, 28; Mintz, *Huck's Raft*, 7–12. See also Demos, *The Unredeemed Captive*.

4. Proverbs 22:15 (Revised Standard Version).

5. Axtell, *The School upon a Hill*, 195.

6. Piele, "Neither Corporal Punishment Cruel nor Due Process Due," 95.

7. Mather, *Help for Distressed Parents*. See also Sutton, *Stubborn Children*; Straus, *Beating the Devil out of Them*.

8. Winslow, "On the Dangerous Tendency to Innovations and Extremes in Education," 184. See also Jewett, "The Fight against Corporal Punishment in American Schools."

9. Ozment, *When Fathers Ruled*, 144, 146–47.

10. Mintz, *Huck's Raft*, 11, 19; Schlesinger, "Cotton Mather and His Children."

11. Piele, "Neither Corporal Punishment Cruel nor Due Process Due," 95.

12. Greven, *The Protestant Temperament*.

13. Hyman and MacDowell, "Introduction," 5.

14. McClellan, *Moral Education in America*, 7.

15. Finkelstein, *Governing the Young*; Butchart, "Punishments, Penalties, Prizes, and Procedures."

16. Axtell, *The School upon a Hill*, 199.

17. Kaestle, "Social Change, Discipline, and the Common School in Early Nineteenth-Century America"; Glenn, "School Discipline and Punishment in Antebellum America"; Jewett, "The Fight against Corporal Punishment in American Schools."

18. Grinspan, *The Virgin Vote*, 24.

19. Zimmerman, *Small Wonder*, 36.

20. West, *Growing Up with the Country*, 203.

21. Grinspan, *The Virgin Vote*, 26.

22. Prince, *School Management and Method*, 60.

23. West, *Growing Up with the Country*, 203.

24. The phrase was offensive enough to provoke violence from the students. See Grose and Clarke, *The 1811 Dictionary of the Vulgar Tongue.*

25. Rentschler, "Applying the Hand of Wisdom to the Seat of Learning," 363.

26. Irving, *The Legend of Sleepy Hollow*, 20.

27. Whitman, "Death in the Schoolroom."

28. Kaestle, *Pillars of the Republic*, 19.

29. Falk, *Corporal Punishment*, 54.

30. Manning, "Discipline in the Good Old Days," 50.

31. See Finkelstein, *Governing the Young*, 214–15, 226.

32. Johnson, *Old Time Schools and School-Books*, 44; Falk, *Corporal Punishment*, 47.

33. Coram, *Political Inquiries*, 94–95; May, "Dedication of a Schoolhouse," 219; Glenn, "School Discipline and Punishment in Antebellum America," 395; Zimmerman, *Small Wonder*, 42.

34. Axtell, *The School upon a Hill*, 194–95.

35. Manning, "Discipline in the Good Old Days," 50.

36. "Farmer Morris's Scarecrow," *Christian Recorder*, August 1, 1868, 1.

37. Falk, *Corporal Punishment*, 54.

38. Falk, 103.

39. Glenn, "School Discipline and Punishment in Antebellum America," 402.

40. Cobb, *The Evil Tendencies of Corporal Punishment*, 84.

41. Theobald, "Country School Curriculum and Governance," 124.

42. Falk, *Corporal Punishment*, 56–57.

43. Falk, 54.

44. Falk, 54, 67, 79–80, 92.

45. Cobb, *The Evil Tendencies of Corporal Punishment*, 80, 254.

46. Falk, *Corporal Punishment*, 94.

47. Glenn, "School Discipline and Punishment in Antebellum America," 406–7.

48. Cobb, *The Evil Tendencies of Corporal Punishment*, 10, 80.

49. Stearns and Stearns, "American Schools and the Uses of Shame," 65.

50. Johnson, *Old Time Schools and School-Books*, 47.

51. Vogler, "The Poor Child's Friend," 4–5.

52. See Tocqueville, *Democracy in America*; Mill, *On Liberty*.

53. See Mendible, *American Shame*.

54. Greven, *The Protestant Temperament*.

55. Locke, *Some Thoughts concerning Education*, 30.

56. Locke, 38–39.

57. Locke, 36.

58. Locke, 33.

59. Baltes, "Locke's Inverted Quarantine," 174; Brady, "Locke's Thoughts on Reputation," 342.

60. Koganzon, "Contesting the Empire of Habit," 548, 551.

61. Hume, *A Treatise of Human Nature*, 602–3.

62. Rush, *The Selected Writings of Benjamin Rush*, 111; Cobb, *The Evil Tendencies of Corporal Punishment*, 230; Glenn, "School Discipline and Punishment in Antebellum America," 406.

63. Hogan, "The Market Revolution and Disciplinary Power"; Opal, "Academies and the Transformation of the Rural North"; Kett, *Merit*.

64. Reese, *Testing Wars in the Public Schools*, chapter 1; Kett, *Merit*; Jonas and Chambers, "The Use and Abuses of Emulation as a Pedagogical Practice."

65. Opal, "Academies and the Transformation of the Rural North," 453, 462.

66. Coram, *Political Inquiries*, 102–3.

67. Upton, "Lancasterian Schools, Republican Citizenship, and the Spatial Imagination."

68. Upton, 239, 243–46.

69. Foucault, *Discipline and Punish*, 172–73, 198.

70. Bentham, *Chrestomathia*; Bentham, *Legislator of the World*, 55–59; quoted in Itzkin, "Bentham's *Chrestomathia*," 308–9.

71. Quoted in Itzkin, "Bentham's *Chrestomathia*," 312.

72. Southey, "Fox, *A Comparative View*," 281; Southey, *The Origin, Nature, and Object, of the New System of Education*, 82–84; Coleridge, *Biographia Literaria*, 60–61; Foakes, "Thriving Prisoners"; Duggett, "Southey's 'New System.'"

73. Kaestle, "Social Change, Discipline, and the Common School in Early Nineteenth-Century America," 2. See also Neem, *Democracy's Schools*, chapter 4.

74. Upton, "Lancasterian Schools, Republican Citizenship, and the Spatial Imagination," 251.

75. Butchart, "Punishments, Penalties, Prizes, and Procedures," 29–30. As noted below, echoes of the Lancaster system persisted far longer in the quasi-militaristic education of Black Americans and Indigenous peoples. See Engs, *Educating the Disfranchised and Disinherited*.

76. Plotz, "The Perpetual Messiah"; Reese, "The Origins of Progressive Education"; Hogan, "Modes of Discipline"; Parille, *Boys at Home*, chapter 4.

77. Halttunen, "Humanitarianism and the Pornography of Pain in Anglo-American Culture"; Pearson, *The Rights of the Defenseless*.

78. Glenn, "School Discipline and Punishment in Antebellum America," 397.

79. Cobb, *The Evil Tendencies of Corporal Punishment*, 79.

80. Glenn, "School Discipline and Punishment in Antebellum America," 401.

81. Cobb, *The Evil Tendencies of Corporal Punishment*, 83.

82. Glenn, "School Discipline and Punishment in Antebellum America," 396; Hogan, "Modes of Discipline," 3.

83. Stearns and Stearns, "American Schools and the Uses of Shame," 61.

84. Neem, *Democracy's Schools*, chapter 1; Stearns and Stearns, "American Schools and the Uses of Shame," 58.

85. Katz, *The Irony of Early School Reform*, part II.

86. Hogan, "Modes of Discipline," 18, referencing Hall, *Lectures on Schoolkeeping for Female Teachers*, 28–29.

87. Wright and Gardner, *Hall's Lectures on School-Keeping*, 115.

88. Hogan, "Modes of Discipline," 19–21, quoting Hall, *Lectures on Schoolkeeping*, 115.

89. Falk, *Corporal Punishment*, 78.

90. Little is known about John Dewey's brief sojourn as a high school teacher in Oil City, Pennsylvania, but it seems unlikely that he employed corporal punishment, given that he was reading Whitman at the time and coming to realize his "oneness with the universe." Westbrook, *John Dewey and American Democracy*, 8.

91. McClellan, *Moral Education in America*, 24. Also see chapters 1, 5, and 7 in Rousmaniere, Dehli, and de Coninck-Smith, *Discipline, Moral Regulation, and Schooling*.

92. Tyack and Hansot, *Learning Together*, 68.

93. Speicher, "The School of One Scholar."

94. Tyack and Hansot, *Learning Together*, 102.

95. Cobb, *The Evil Tendencies of Corporal Punishment*, 11.

96. Tyack and Hansot, *Learning Together*, 91–92.

97. Falk, *Corporal Punishment*, 59.

98. Alcott, *Little Women*, 131–35.

99. Theobald, *Call School*, 131.

100. Tyack and Hansot, *Learning Together*, 68.

101. Emerson, *The Complete Writings*, 993.

102. Armistead, *Anthony Benezet*, 8.

103. Altfest, *Robert Owen as Educator*, 55–56.

104. Dahlstrand, *Amos Bronson Alcott*, 39, 42–43, 94–95.

105. Glenn, "School Discipline and Punishment in Antebellum America," 403.

106. Jones, *Soldiers of Light and Love*, 125; Butchart, *Schooling the Freed People*, 134–35, 155; Stevenson, *The Victorian Homefront*, 88.

107. For an example from freedmen's schools, see Sarah Chase to Fred W. May, Charleston, December 7, 1866, in *Northern Visions of Race, Region & Reform*, American Antiquarian Society, http://www.americanantiquarian.org/Freedmen/Manuscripts/Chase/12-07-1866.html.

108. Adams, *Education for Extinction*, 121–24.

109. Bagley, *Classroom Management*, 117–18. The notion of ontogenic recapitulation originated with the German biologist Ernst Haeckel. See Haeckel, *The Riddle of the Universe*, 81. On the persistence of punishment in schools, see Stearns and Stearns, "American Schools and the Uses of Shame," 59–60.

110. Historians of school reform have often noted the conservatism of school organization and culture. See Cuban, *How Teachers Taught*; Cohen and Mehta, "Why Reform Sometimes Succeeds."

111. Falk, *Corporal Punishment*, 69.

112. Butchart, "Introduction," 8.

113. Chamberlain, *The Child*, 389, quoting Hall, "Moral Training and Will-Training," 82.

114. James, *Talks to Teachers on Psychology*, 53.

Chapter Three

1. Link, *The Paradox of Southern Progressivism, 1880–1930.*

2. Lee, *To Kill a Mockingbird*, 30–31.

3. On the evolution of professionalization in teaching, see Mehta, *The Allure of Order*, chapters 1–2.

4. On medicalization and therapy, see Cohen, "The Mental Hygiene Movement, the Development of Personality and the School"; and Petrina, "The Medicalization of Education." On the difficulty of documenting classroom practices, see Zilversmit, *Changing Schools*; and Cuban, *How Teachers Taught*.

5. Labaree, *The Trouble with Ed Schools*.

6. Woolfolk, *The Value of Psychotherapy*, 3–5; Ryan, "From Rod to Reason," 75.

7. Butchart, "Punishments, Penalties, Prizes, and Procedures," 36.

8. Weaver, "Education and the Individual"; Arendt, "The Crisis in Education."

9. Hartman, *Education and the Cold War*, chapter 3.

10. Carson, *The Measure of Merit*; Schneider, *From the Ivory Tower to the Schoolhouse*. Although it goes beyond the scope of our inquiry, one sees the same trend with the proliferation of aptitude and personality tests following World War II.

11. Maslow, "A Theory of Human Motivation."

12. Addicott, *Constructive Classroom Control*, 12–13.

13. Butchart, "Punishments, Penalties, Prizes, and Procedures," 33; Erich Fromm, "Foreword," in Neill, *Summerhill*, x.

14. Cohen, "In the Name of the Prevention of Neurosis"; McClay, *The Masterless*.

15. Amsterdam, *Constructive Classroom Discipline and Practice*, 72, 89; Addicott, *Constructive Classroom Control*, 4. As Ann Hulbert explains, it was during the early twentieth century that educators and other child-service providers sought to establish their professional expertise by denigrating parents. Hulbert, *Raising America*.

16. Quoted in Igo, *The Known Citizen*, 129–31.

17. Igo, *The Known Citizen*, 129–31.

18. Adorno, "Education after Auschwitz."

19. Bagley, *Classroom Management*, 102, 106–7.

20. Woolfolk, *The Value of Psychotherapy*, 29–33; Skinner, *Walden Two*; Skinner, *Beyond Freedom and Dignity*.

21. Rhode, *Armed with Expertise*.

22. Bagley, *Classroom Management*, 102, 106–7.

23. Amsterdam, *Constructive Classroom Discipline and Practice*, 70–71.

24. For a quick discussion of total environments in education, see Peshkin, *God's Choice*.

25. We omit discussion of many of these systems, including values clarification, Teacher Effectiveness Training, transactional analysis, and others. See Glickman and Wolfgang, *Solving Discipline Problems*.

26. Canter, *Assertive Discipline*.

27. Glasser, *Schools without Failure*.

28. Glasser, *Control Theory*, 32.

29. See, for instance, Kellogg, *School Management*; Baldwin, *The Art of School Management*; White, *School Management*; Taylor, *Art of Class Management and Discipline*; and Dutton, *School Management*.

30. Tyack, *The One Best System*; Strober and Tyack, "Why Do Women Teach and Men Manage?"; Lippmann, *Drift and Mastery*.

31. Ravitch, *Left Back*, 45.

32. Mirel, "The Traditional High School."

33. Tropea, "Bureaucratic Order and Special Children," 44.

34. Tropea, 37–38.

35. Kafka, *The History of "Zero Tolerance" in American Public Schooling*, 55.

36. Rousmaniere, *The Principal's Office*, 55.

37. Grant, *The Boy Problem*; Tropea, "Bureaucratic Order and Special Children"; Shulman, "Crime Prevention and the Public Schools," 80.

38. Duke and Jones, "Two Decades of Discipline"; Bayh, *Our Nation's Schools—A Report Card*; "School Violence and Vandalism," 1975, series 29, box 1746, folder 7, National Education Association Archives, George Washington University.

39. Hutt, *A Brief History of the Student Record*.

40. Igo, *The Known Citizen*, 250–53.

41. Tanenhaus, *The Constitutional Rights of Children*.

42. Igo, *The Known Citizen*, 250.

43. Agyepong, *The Criminalization of Black Children*, 1, 59, 64.

44. Lyons, *Teachers and Reform*, 146–49.

45. Perrillo, *Uncivil Rights*; Kozol, *Death at an Early Age*.

46. Bailey, *Disruption in Urban Secondary Schools*.

47. *A Profile of Large City Schools* (National Assn. Secondary School Principals, 1970), 9, series 40, box 4207, folder 1, National Education Association Archives.

48. Jack Slater, "Death of a School," *Phi Delta Kappan*, December 1974, series 47, box 1913, folder 17, National Education Association Archives.

49. Little Rock Classroom Teachers Association Report, n.d., series 47, box 2761, file 2, National Education Association Archives.

50. *Vandalism and Violence: Innovative Strategies Reduce Cost to Schools*, A Publication of the National School Public Relations Association, Vandalism and Violence (1971), 44, series 40, box 4207, folder 1, National Education Association Archives.

51. Ben Brodinsky, *Student Discipline: Problems and Solutions*, AASA Critical Issues Report (1980), 72, series 40, box 274, folder 9, National Education Association Archives.

52. "Boys Prepare Survey of Teachers," *New York Times*, December 30, 1942; Jostyn, "The Manhasset Youth Council"; Stein, "Adolescent Participation in Community Co-ordinating Councils"; Drinan, *The War on Kids*, 47.

53. For contemporary discussions of school policing, see Nolan, *Police in the Hallways*; Mukherjee, *Criminalizing the Classroom*; Rios, *Punished*; and Kupchik and Bracy, "To Protect, Serve, and Mentor?"

54. Black Education Commission, "Racism, Repression, and Inefficiency in the Deployment and Practices of School Security," July 30, 1979, collection 1923, box 1460, Los Angeles Unified School District Records, UCLA Archives; Brede, "The Policing of Juveniles in Chicago."

55. Hinton, "A War within Our Own Boundaries," 107; Levitan and Taggart, "The Emergency Employment Act"; Superintendent William J. Johnston to John A. Simpson, April 16, 1974, collection 1923, box 1459, Los Angeles Unified School District Records.

56. "School Violence and Vandalism," 1975, series 29, box 1746, folder 7, National Education Association Archives.

57. Pierce v. Society of Sisters, 268 U.S. 510 (1925).

58. Provasnik, "Judicial Activism and the Origins of Parental Choice," 312–13; Steffes, *School, Society, and State*, 120.

59. Scribner, *The Fight for Local Control*, chapter 4.

60. Our argument here follows MacIntyre, "How to Seem Virtuous without Actually Being So."

61. Driver, *The Schoolhouse Gate*, 142. See also Schumaker, *Troublemakers*; Arum and Preiss, "Still Judging School Discipline."

62. Gideon v. Wainwright, 372 U.S. 335 (1963); Miranda v. Arizona, 384 U.S. 436 (1966).

63. Kent v. United States, 383 U.S. 541 (1966); In re Gault, 387 U.S. 1 (1967).

64. Tinker v. Des Moines, 393 U.S. 503, 506 (1969).

65. *Tinker*, 393 U.S. at 508.

66. Goss v. Lopez, 419 U.S. 565, 580 (1975).

67. *Lopez*, 419 U.S. at 585.

68. *Lopez*, 419 U.S. at 575, 589; Kupchik, *The Real School Safety Problem*.

69. *Lopez*, 419 U.S. at 598 n.19.

70. Lee, "A Legal Analysis of *Ingraham v. Wright*."

71. Ingraham v. Wright, 430 U.S. 651 (1977); Renteln, "Corporal Punishment and the Cultural Defense."

72. *Ingraham*, 430 U.S. at 677–78, 700.

73. Cooper v. McJunkin, 4 Ind. 290, 293 (1853).

74. *Ingraham*, 430 U.S. at 684 n.1; Falk, *Corporal Punishment*, 89; Rentschler, "Applying the Hand of Wisdom to the Seat of Learning," 362.

75. *Ingraham*, 430 U.S. at 662.

76. American Civil Liberties Union, *A Violent Education*, 5.

77. Friedman and Hyman, "Corporal Punishment in the Schools," 164–66.

78. Ware v. Estes, 328 F. Supp. 657 (1971).

79. Friedman and Hyman, "Corporal Punishment in the Schools," 162.

80. Friedman and Hyman, 177.

81. Friedman and Hyman, 163; Rolando v. School Directors of District No. 125, County of LaSalle, 358 N.E.2d 945 (Ill. App. Ct. 1976).

82. Sarah Gonzalez, "Spanking Lives on in Rural Florida Schools," National Public Radio, March 13, 2012, http://www.npr.org/2012/03/13/148521155/spanking-lives-on-in-rural-florida-schools.

83. Hall v. Tawney, 621 F.2d 607 (1980); Garcia v. Miera, 817 F.2d 650 (1987). For a more recent case, see Johnson v. Newburgh Enlarged School District, 239 F.3d 246 (2d Cir. 2001).

84. Weiss, "Curbing Violence or Teaching It."

85. Pierson v. Ray, 386 U.S. 547 (1967); Harlow v. Fitzgerald, 457 U.S. 800 (1982).

86. Serafin v. School of Excellence in Education, 252 Fed. Appx. 684, 685 (2007).

87. Ad Hoc Corporal Punishment Committee, "Corporal Punishment in Schools."

88. See, for instance, Afifi et al., "Physical Punishment and Mental Disorders."

89. Human Rights Watch/ACLU, *Impairing Education*, 43.

90. Human Rights Watch/ACLU, 43–44.

91. Ohene et al., "Parental Expectations, Physical Punishment, and Violence among Adolescents Who Score Positive on a Psychosocial Screening Test in Primary Care."

92. Brooks, "Does Philosophy Deserve a Place at the Supreme Court?"; Superfine, "The Evolving Role of the Courts in Educational Policy."

93. For examples, see Gershoff, "School Corporal Punishment in Global Perspective"; Glaser, "Nostalgia for a Beating"; Tafa, "Corporal Punishment."

94. Wexler, "Defending the Middle Way," 300.

95. Pettinga, "Rational Basis with Bite," 783.

96. This was exactly the point raised in dissenting opinions in *Ingraham v. Wright* at the appellate level. See Ingraham v. Wright, 525 F.2d 909, 917 (5th Cir. 1976).

97. Brown v. Board of Education of Topeka, 347 U.S. 483, 493 (1954); San Antonio Independent School District v. Rodriguez, 411 U.S. 1 (1973).

98. Plyler v. Doe, 457 U.S. 202, 244 (1982).

99. Wexler, "Defending the Middle Way," 300, 322, 338.

100. Schapiro, "Polyphonic Federalism."

101. See, for example, United States v. Virginia, 518 U.S. 515 (1996); Grutter v. Bollinger, 539 U.S. 306 (2003); and Fisher v. University of Texas, 570 U.S. 297 (2013). For a similar intermediate standard applied to gender discrimination (the "substantial relation" test), see Craig v. Boren, 429 U.S. 190 (1976).

102. This was essentially the approach taken in Serrano v. Priest, 5 Cal. 3d 584 (1971), a landmark school-funding case. "Education Law—School Finance"; Pettinga, "Rational Basis with Bite"; Barrett, "The Rational Basis Standard"; Neily, "One Test, Two Standards."

103. Arum, *Judging School Discipline*, 201.

104. Bennett, DiIulio, and Walter, *Body Count*, 27.

105. Bennett, DiIulio, and Walter, 47–48.

106. Kim, Losen, and Hewitt, *The School-to-Prison Pipeline*; Meek, "School Discipline 'As Part of the Teaching Process'"; Ferguson, *Bad Boys*; Raby, *School Rules*.

107. United States Government Accountability Office, *Discipline Disparities for Black Students, Boys, and Students with Disabilities*, 3.

108. Gregory, Skiba, and Noguera, "The Achievement Gap and the Discipline Gap," 60–63.

109. Petrilli, "A Supposed Discipline Fix Threatens School Cultures"; United States Government Accountability Office, *Discipline Disparities for Black Students, Boys, and Students with Disabilities*.

110. Moriah Balingit, "Racial Disparities in School Discipline Are Growing, Federal Data Show," *Washington Post*, April 24, 2018, https://www.washingtonpost.com/local/education/racial-disparities-in-school-discipline-are-growing-federal-data-shows/2018/04/24/67b5d2b8-47e4-11e8-827e-190efaf1f1ee_story.html.

111. Skiba et al., "What Do We Know about Discipline Disparities?," 24.

112. Goff et al., "The Essence of Innocence," 526.

113. Gilliam et al., *Do Early Educators' Implicit Biases Regarding Sex and Race Relate to Behavior Expectations?*

114. Skiba et al., "What Do We Know about Discipline Disparities?," 25.

115. Noltemeyer and Ward, "Relationship between School Suspension and Student Outcomes"; Losen and Skiba, *Suspended Education*, 1, 6; Fabelo et al., *Breaking Schools' Rules*.

116. For a list of citations, see Losen and Skiba, *Suspended Education*, 9.

117. Eden, *School Discipline Reform and Disorder*, 10.

118. Curran, "The Law, Policy, and Portrayal of Zero Tolerance School Discipline"; Skiba, Shure, and Williams, *What Do We Know about Racial and Ethnic Disproportionality in School Suspension and Expulsion?*; Gordon, "Disproportionality in Student Discipline."

119. Eden, *School Discipline Reform and Disorder*, 9.

120. Redfield and Nance, *School-to-Prison Pipeline*.

121. McGrew, "The Dangers of Pipeline Thinking," 348. See also Crawley and Hirschfield, "Examining the School-to-Prison Pipeline Metaphor"; McGrew, *Education's Prisoners*.

122. McGrew, "The Dangers of Pipeline Thinking," 350.

123. McGrew, 355–56.

124. McGrew, 354.

125. Under modern conditions, physical punishment is replaced by controlling people "from the inside," making them feel constantly watched. Individuals eventually come to embody the values of the existing power structure (Foucault calls this process "dynamic normalization"). Foucault, *Discipline and Punish*, 184, 227–28, 293–308.

126. Curran, "The Law, Policy, and Portrayal of Zero Tolerance School Discipline," 338–42; Losen and Skiba, *Suspended Education*, 10.

127. Here, our argument about schools is broadly similar to William Stuntz's argument about the criminal writ large, in which he calls for less punitive laws, less discretion on the part of prosecutors, and greater opportunities for leniency in the deliberations of jurors. See Stuntz, *The Collapse of American Criminal Justice*, chapter 10.

Chapter Four

1. Brennan and Noggle, "The Moral Status of Children," 7.

2. Brennan and Noggle, 6.

3. Tinker v. Des Moines, 393 U.S. 503, 506 (1969).

4. Bethel School District No. 403 v. Fraser, 478 U.S. 675 (1986); Hazelwood School District v. Kuhlmeier, 484 U.S. 260 (1988); Morse v. Frederick, 551 U.S. 393 (2007).

5. For additional discussion of the role of institutional context in constitutional law, see Schauer, "Towards an Institutional First Amendment."

6. For a detailed description of the full set of the special characteristics of schools, see Warnick, *Understanding Student Rights in Schools.*

7. Robles, "Executive Perceptions of the Top 10 Soft Skills Needed in Today's Workplace." Here, vocational education begins to overlap with civic education, because a vocational education should not only help students learn how to work together but also give students a sense of being equal to others within the democratic polis by giving them an equal chance at obtaining desirable social positions and social goods through their employment.

8. Mitchell, Skinner, and White, "Essential Soft Skills for Success in the Twenty-First Century Workforce as Perceived by Business Educators."

9. Brighouse, *On Education*; Callan, *Creating Citizens*; Levinson, *The Demands of Liberal Education*; Newman, *Realizing Educational Rights*; Reich, *Bridging Liberalism and Multiculturalism in American Education.*

10. Galston, *Liberal Purposes.*

11. Hand, "Against Autonomy as an Educational Aim."

12. Neill, *Summerhill*, 124.

13. Noguera, "Schools, Prisons, and Social Implications of Punishment," 347.

14. Morrison and Vaandering, "Restorative Justice," 140.

15. Council on School Health, "Out-of-School Suspension and Expulsion," e1001.

16. Noguera, "Schools, Prisons, and Social Implications of Punishment," 346.

17. Canton, *Why Punish?*, 153.

18. Sherman and Strang, *Restorative Justice.*

19. Zehr, *Changing Lenses.*

20. Sherman and Strang, "Empathy for the Devil."

21. Tavuchis, *Mea Culpa*, 5.

22. Canton, *Why Punish?*, 166.

23. Roberts and Stalans, "Restorative Sentencing."

24. Braithwaite, "Values and Restorative Justice in Schools," 138.

25. Brooks, *Punishment*, 72.

26. Canton, *Why Punish?*, 152.

27. Brooks, *Punishment*, 72.

28. Quoted in Patrick O'Donnell, "The Ins and Outs of 'Restorative Justice' in Schools," *The Educated Reporter* (blog), Education Writers Association, April 12, 2018, https://www.ewa.org /blog-educated-reporter/ins-and-outs-restorative-justice-schools.

29. Macready, "Learning Social Responsibility in Schools."

30. McCluskey et al., "Can Restorative Practices in Schools Make a Difference?"

31. Bennett, *The Apology Ritual*, 9.

32. Paul Sperry, "How Liberal Discipline Policies Are Making Schools Less Safe," *New York Post*, March 14, 2015, https://nypost.com/2015/03/14/politicians-are-making-schools-less-safe -and-ruining-education-for-everyone/.

33. Max Eden, "Restorative Justice Isn't Working, But That's Not What the Media Is Reporting," Fordham Institute, January 14, 2019, https://fordhaminstitute.org/national/commentary /restorative-justice-isnt-working-thats-not-what-media-reporting.

34. Fronius et al., *Restorative Justice in U.S. Schools*, 26.

35. Augustine et al., *Can Restorative Practices Improve School Climate and Curb Suspensions?*; Acosta et al., "Evaluation of a Whole-School Change Intervention."

36. Joie D. Acosta, Catherine H. Augustine, Matthew Chinman, and John Engberg, "What Two New Studies Reveal about Restorative Justice in Middle School and How It Can Be Done Better," *The RAND Blog*, Rand Corporation, April 17, 2019, https://www.rand.org/blog/2019/04 /what-two-new-studies-reveal-about-restorative-justice.html.

37. One approach that was the focus in the RAND studies was the International Institute for Restorative Practices' Whole-School Change program. Even within this one general approach, some variation is possible, such as who runs the restorative conferences and when, and what each conference looks like. Programs can vary according to how they are implemented, their breadth of focus, their professional development approach, and the resources and time they dedicate to the endeavor. A restorative justice approach can also be paired (or not) with other behavioral interventions such as the Positive Behavioral Interventions and Supports program.

38. Anfara, Evans, and Lester, "Restorative Justice in Education."

39. Lustick, "'Restorative Justice' or Restoring Order?"; Madison Teachers Incorporated, *Joint Committee on Safety and Discipline.*

40. Jain et al., *Restorative Justice in Oakland Schools.*

Bibliography

Court Decisions

Bethel School District No. 403 v. Fraser, 478 U.S. 675 (1986).

Brown v. Board of Education of Topeka, 347 U.S. 483 (1954).

Cooper v. McJunkin, 4 Ind. 290 (1853).

Craig v. Boren, 429 U.S. 190 (1976).

Fisher v. University of Texas, 570 U.S. 297 (2013).

Garcia v. Miera, 817 F.2d 650 (1987).

Gideon v. Wainwright, 372 U.S. 335 (1963).

Goss v. Lopez, 419 U.S. 565 (1975).

Grutter v. Bollinger, 539 U.S. 306 (2003).

Hall v. Tawney, 621 F.2d 607 (1980).

Harlow v. Fitzgerald, 457 U.S. 800 (1982).

Hazelwood School District v. Kuhlmeier, 484 U.S. 260 (1988).

Ingraham v. Wright, 430 U.S. 651 (1977).

Ingraham v. Wright, 525 F.2d 909, 917 (5th Cir. 1976).

In re Gault, 387 U.S. 1 (1967).

Johnson v. Newburgh Enlarged School District, 239 F.3d 246 (2d Cir. 2001).

Kent v. United States, 383 U.S. 541 (1966).

Miranda v. Arizona, 384 U.S. 436 (1966).

Morse v. Frederick, 551 U.S. 393 (2007).

Pierce v. Society of Sisters, 268 U.S. 510 (1925).

Pierson v. Ray, 386 U.S. 547 (1967).

Plyler v. Doe, 457 U.S. 202 (1982).

Rolando v. School Directors of District No. 125, County of LaSalle, 358 N.E.2d 945 (Ill. App. Ct. 1976).

San Antonio Independent School District v. Rodriguez, 411 U.S. 1 (1973).

Scott v. County of San Bernardino, 903 F.3d 943 (2018).

Serafin v. School of Excellence in Education, 252 Fed. Appx. 684 (2007).

Serrano v. Priest, 5 Cal. 3d 584 (1971).

S.G. ex rel. A.G. v. Sayreville Bd. of Education, 333 F.3d 417 (3d Cir. 2003).

Tinker v. Des Moines Independent Community School District, 393 U.S. 503 (1969).

United States v. Virginia, 518 U.S. 515 (1996).

Ware v. Estes, 328 F. Supp. 657 (1971).

Primary and Secondary Sources

Acosta, Joie, Matthew Chinman, Patricia Ebener, Patrick S. Malone, Andrea Phillips, and Asa Waks. "Evaluation of a Whole-School Change Intervention: Findings from a Two-Year Cluster Randomized Trial of the Restorative Practices Intervention." *Journal of Youth and Adolescence* 48, no. 5 (2019): 876–90.

Adams, David Wallace. *Education for Extinction: American Indians and the Boarding School Experience, 1875–1928*. Lawrence: University Press of Kansas, 1995.

Addicott, Irwin O. *Constructive Classroom Control*. San Francisco: Howard Chandler, 1958.

Ad Hoc Corporal Punishment Committee. "Corporal Punishment in Schools: Position Paper of the Society for Adolescent Medicine." *Journal of Adolescent Health* 32, no. 5 (2003): 385–93.

Adorno, Theodor W. "Education after Auschwitz." In *Can One Live after Auschwitz? A Philosophical Reader*, edited by Rolf Tiedemann, 19–33. Stanford: Stanford University Press, 2003.

Afifi, Tracie O., Natalie P. Mota, Patricia Dasiewicz, Harriet L. MacMillan, and Jitender Sareen. "Physical Punishment and Mental Disorders: Results from a Nationally Representative US Sample." *Pediatrics* 130, no. 2 (August 2012): 184–92.

Agyepong, Tera E. *The Criminalization of Black Children: Race, Gender, and Delinquency in Chicago's Juvenile Justice System*. Chapel Hill: University of North Carolina Press, 2018.

Alcott, Louisa May. *Little Women*. New York: World Publishing Company, 1969.

Altfest, Karen. *Robert Owen as Educator*. Boston: Twayne Publishers, 1977.

American Civil Liberties Union. *A Violent Education: Corporal Punishment of Children in U.S. Public Schools*. American Civil Liberties Union, 2009.

Amsterdam, Ruth. *Constructive Classroom Discipline and Practice*. New York: Comet Press, 1957.

Anfara, Vincent A., Jr., Katherine R. Evans, and Jessica N. Lester. "Restorative Justice in Education: What We Know So Far." *Middle School Journal* 44, no. 5 (2013): 57–63.

Arendt, Hannah. "The Crisis in Education." In *Between Past and Future: Eight Exercises in Political Thought*, 173–96. New York: Viking Press, 1968.

Armistead, Wilson. *Anthony Benezet: From the Original Memoir*. Philadelphia: Lippincott, 1859.

Arum, Richard. *Judging School Discipline: The Crisis of Moral Authority*. Cambridge, MA: Harvard University Press, 2003.

Arum, Richard, and Doreet Preiss. "Still Judging School Discipline." In *From Schoolhouse to Courthouse: The Judiciary's Role in American Education*, edited by Joshua M. Dunn and Martin R. West, 238–60. Washington, DC: Brookings Institution Press, 2009.

Augustine. *The Confessions*. Translated by R. S. Pinecoffin. London: Penguin Books, 1961.

Augustine, Catherine H., John Engberg, Geoffrey E. Grimm, Emma Lee, Elaine Lin Wang, Karen Christianson, and Andrea A. Joseph. *Can Restorative Practices Improve School Climate and Curb Suspensions? An Evaluation of the Impact of Restorative Practices in a Mid-Sized Urban School District*. Santa Monica, CA: RAND Corporation, 2018. https://www.rand.org/pubs/research_reports/RR2840.html.

Axtell, James. *The School upon a Hill: Education and Society in Colonial New England*. New York: Norton, 1976.

Bagley, William Chandler. *Classroom Management: Its Principles and Technique*. New York: MacMillan, 1921.

Bailey, Beth. *From Front Porch to Back Seat: Courtship in Twentieth-Century America*. Baltimore: Johns Hopkins University Press, 1988.

Bailey, Stephen K. *Disruption in Urban Secondary Schools*. Washington, DC: National Association of Secondary School Principals, 1970.

Bailyn, Bernard. *Education in the Forming of American Society*. Chapel Hill: University of North Carolina Press, 1960.

Baldwin, Joseph. *The Art of School Management*. Toronto: Gage, 1885.

Baltes, John. "Locke's Inverted Quarantine: Discipline, Panopticism, and the Making of the Liberal Subject." *Review of Politics* 75, no. 3 (2013): 173–92.

Barrett, Edward L. "The Rational Basis Standard for Equal Protection Review of Ordinary Legislative Classifications." *Kentucky Law Journal* 68, no. 4 (1979): 845–78.

Bayh, Birch. *Our Nation's Schools—A Report Card: "A" in School Violence and Vandalism*. Washington, DC: US Government Printing Office, 1976.

Benn, S. I. "An Approach to the Problems of Punishment." *Philosophy* 33, no. 127 (1958): 325–41.

Bennett, Christopher. *The Apology Ritual: A Philosophical Theory of Punishment*. Cambridge: Cambridge University Press, 2010.

Bennett, William J., John J. DiIulio, and John P. Walter. *Body Count: Moral Poverty and How to Win America's War against Crime and Drugs*. New York: Simon & Schuster, 1996.

Bentham, Jeremy. *Chrestomathia*. Edited by M. J. Smith and W. H. Burston. Oxford: Clarendon Press, 1983.

Bentham, Jeremy. *"Legislator of the World": Writings on Codification, Law, and Education*. Edited by Philip Schofield and Jonathan Harris. Oxford: Clarendon Press, 1998.

Boonin, David. *The Problem of Punishment*. Cambridge: Cambridge University Press, 2008.

Brady, Michelle E. "Locke's Thoughts on Reputation." *Review of Politics* 75, no. 3 (2013): 335–56.

Braithwaite, Valerie. "Values and Restorative Justice in Schools." In *Restorative Justice: Philosophy to Practice*, edited by Heather Strang and John Braithwaite, 121–44. Aldershot, UK: Ashgate, 2000.

Brede, Richard M. "The Policing of Juveniles in Chicago." PhD diss., University of Illinois, 1971.

Brennan, Samantha, and Robert Noggle. "The Moral Status of Children: Children's Rights, Parents' Rights, and Family Justice." *Social Theory and Practice* 23, no. 1 (1997): 1–26.

Brighouse, Harry. *On Education*. London: Routledge, 2006.

Brooks, Thom. "Does Philosophy Deserve a Place at the Supreme Court?" *Rutgers Law Record* 27 (2003): 1–17.

Brooks, Thom. *Punishment*. Abingdon, Oxon: Routledge, 2012.

Butchart, Ronald E. "Introduction." In Butchart and McEwan, *Classroom Discipline in American Schools*, 1–18.

Butchart, Ronald E. "Punishments, Penalties, Prizes, and Procedures: A History of Discipline in U.S. Schools." In Butchart and McEwan, *Classroom Discipline in American Schools*, 19–50.

Butchart, Ronald E. *Schooling the Freed People: Teaching, Learning, and the Struggle for Black Freedom, 1861–1876*. Chapel Hill: University of North Carolina Press, 2010.

Butchart, Ronald E., and Barbara McEwan, eds. *Classroom Discipline in American Schools: Problems and Possibilities for Democratic Education*. Albany: State University of New York Press, 1998.

Callan, Eammon. *Creating Citizens: Political Education and Liberal Democracy*. Oxford: Clarendon Press, 1997.

Canter, Lee. *Assertive Discipline: A Take Charge Approach for Today's Educator*. Santa Monica, CA: Canter & Associates, 1976.

Canton, Rob. *Why Punish?: An Introduction to the Philosophy of Punishment*. London: Palgrave, 2017.

Carson, John. *The Measure of Merit: Talents, Intelligence, and Inequality in the French and American Republics, 1750–1940*. Princeton, NJ: Princeton University Press, 2007.

Chamberlain, Alexander Francis. *The Child: A Study in the Evolution of Man*. New York: Scribner, 1917.

Cobb, Lyman. *The Evil Tendencies of Corporal Punishment as a Means of Moral Discipline in Families and Schools*. New York: Mark H. Newman, 1847.

Cohen, David K., and Jal D. Mehta. "Why Reform Sometimes Succeeds: Understanding the Conditions That Produce Reforms That Last." *American Educational Research Journal* 54, no. 4 (August 2017): 644–90.

Cohen, Sol. "In the Name of the Prevention of Neurosis." In Finkelstein, *Regulated Children, Liberated Children*, 184–219.

Cohen, Sol. "The Mental Hygiene Movement, the Development of Personality and the School: Medicalization of American Education." *History of Education Quarterly* 23, no. 2 (Summer 1983): 123–49.

Coleridge, Samuel Taylor. *Biographia Literaria*. Edited by James Engell and W. Jackson Bate. 2 vols. Princeton: Princeton University Press, 1983.

Coram, Robert. *Political Inquiries*. Wilmington, DE: Andrews & Drynberg, 1791.

Council on School Health. "Out-of-School Suspension and Expulsion." *Pediatrics* 131, no. 3 (March 2013): e1000–e1007.

Crawley, Kayla, and Paul Hirschfield. "Examining the School-to-Prison Pipeline Metaphor." In *Oxford Research Encyclopedia of Criminology*, edited by Henry N. Pontell. New York: Oxford University Press, 2018. https://oxfordre.com/criminology/view/10.1093/acrefore/97801 90264079.001.0001/acrefore-9780190264079-e-346.

Crenshaw, Kimberlé, Jyoti Nanda, and Priscilla Ocen. *Black Girls Matter: Pushed Out, Overpoliced, and Underprotected*. New York: Center for Intersectionality and Social Policy Studies, Columbia University, 2015.

Cuban, Larry. *How Teachers Taught: Constancy and Change in American Classrooms, 1890–1990*. New York: Teachers College Press, 1993.

Curran, F. Chris. "The Law, Policy, and Portrayal of Zero Tolerance School Discipline: Examining Prevalence and Characteristics across Levels of Governance and School Districts." *Educational Policy* 33, no. 2 (2019): 319–49.

Dahlstrand, Frederick C. *Amos Bronson Alcott: An Intellectual Biography*. Rutherford, NJ: Fairleigh Dickinson University Press, 1982.

de Brey, Cristobal, Lauren Musu, Joel McFarland, Sidney Wilkinson-Flicker, Melissa Diliberti, Anlan Zhang, Claire Branstetter, and Xiaolei Wang. *Status and Trends in the Education of Racial and Ethnic Groups 2018*. Washington, DC: US Department of Education, 2019.

Demos, John. *The Unredeemed Captive: A Family Story from Early America*. New York: Vintage Books, 1995.

Drinan, Cara. *The War on Kids: How American Juvenile Justice Lost Its Way*. New York: Oxford University Press, 2018.

Driver, Justin. *The Schoolhouse Gate: Public Education, the Supreme Court, and the Battle for the American Mind*. New York: Pantheon Books, 2018.

Duff, Antony. *Punishment, Communication, and Community*. Oxford: Oxford University Press, 2001.

Duggett, Tom. "Southey's 'New System': The Monitorial Controversy and the Making of the 'Entire Man of Letters.'" *Érudit* 61 (April 2012): 1–31. https://www.erudit.org/fr/revues/ravon/2012-n61-ravon0834/1018603ar/.

Duke, Daniel L., and Vernon F. Jones. "Two Decades of Discipline—Assessing the Development of an Educational Specialization." *Journal of Research and Development in Education* 17, no. 4 (1984): 25–35.

Dutton, Samuel Train. *School Management*. New York: Scribner, 1904.

Eden, Max. *School Discipline Reform and Disorder: Evidence from New York City Public Schools, 2012–2016*. New York: Manhattan Institute, 2017.

"Education Law—School Finance—Colorado Supreme Court Upholds State's School Finance System as Rationally Related to the 'Thorough and Uniform' Mandate of the Colorado Constitution's Education Clause." *Harvard Law Review* 127, no. 2 (December 2013): 803–10.

Emerson, Ralph Waldo. *The Complete Writings*. New York: W. H. Wise, 1930.

Engs, Robert Francis. *Educating the Disfranchised and Disinherited: Samuel Chapman Armstrong and Hampton Institute, 1839–1893*. Knoxville: University of Tennessee Press, 1999.

Ezorsky, Gertrude, ed. *Philosophical Perspectives on Punishment*. Albany: State University of New York Press, 1972.

Fabelo, Tony, Michael D. Thompson, Martha Plotkin, Dottie Carmichael, Miner P. Marchbanks III, and Eric A. Booth. *Breaking Schools' Rules: A Statewide Study of How School Discipline Relates to Students' Success and Juvenile Justice Involvement*. New York: Justice Center, Council of State Governments, July 2011.

Falk, Herbert Arnold. *Corporal Punishment: A Social Interpretation of Its Theory and Practice in the Schools of the United States*. New York: Teachers College Press, 1941.

Feinberg, Joel. "The Expressive Function of Punishment." *The Monist* 49, no. 3 (1965): 397–423.

Ferguson, Ann Arnett. *Bad Boys: Public Schools in the Making of Black Masculinity*. Ann Arbor: University of Michigan Press, 2001.

Finkelstein, Barbara. *Governing the Young: Teacher Behavior in Popular Primary Schools in Nineteenth-Century United States*. New York: Falmer Press, 1989.

Finkelstein, Barbara, ed. *Regulated Children, Liberated Children: Education in Psychohistorical Perspective*. New York: Psychohistory Press, 1979.

Flew, Antony. "The Justification of Punishment." *Philosophy* 29, no. 111 (1954): 291–307.

Foakes, R. A. "'Thriving Prisoners': Coleridge, Wordsworth, and the Child at School." *Studies in Romanticism* 28, no. 2 (Summer 1989): 187–206.

Foucault, Michel. *Discipline and Punish: The Birth of the Prison*. New York: Vintage Books, 1995.

Friedman, Robert H., and Irwin A. Hyman. "Corporal Punishment in the Schools." In Hyman and Wise, *Corporal Punishment in American Education*, 157–68.

Fronius, Trevor, Hannah Sutherland, Sarah Guckenburg, Nancy Hurley, and Anthony Petrosino. *Restorative Justice in U.S. Schools: A Research Review*. San Francisco: WestEd Justice and Prevention Research Center, 2016. https://jprc.wested.org/wp-content/uploads/2016/02/RJ_Literature-Review_20160217.pdf.

Galston, William. *Liberal Purposes: Goods, Virtues, and Diversity in the Liberal State*. Cambridge: Cambridge University Press, 1991.

Garland, David. *Punishment and Modern Society: A Study in Social Theory*. Chicago: University of Chicago Press, 1993.

Gershoff, Elizabeth T. "More Harm Than Good: A Summary of Scientific Research on the Intended and Unintended Effects of Corporal Punishment on Children." *Law and Contemporary Problems* 73, no. 2 (2010): 31–56.

Gershoff, Elizabeth T. "School Corporal Punishment in Global Perspective: Prevalence, Outcomes, and Efforts at Intervention." *Psychology, Health & Medicine* 22, sup. 1 (2017): 224–39.

Gershoff, Elizabeth T., and Sarah A. Font. "Corporal Punishment in U.S. Public Schools: Prevalence, Disparities in Use, and Status in State and Federal Policy." *Social Policy Report* 30, no. 1 (2016): 1–25.

Gershoff, Elizabeth T., Kelly M. Purtell, and Igor Holas. *Corporal Punishment in U.S. Public Schools: Legal Precedents, Current Practices, and Future Policy.* New York: Springer, 2015.

Gershoff, Elizabeth Thompson. "Corporal Punishment by Parents and Associated Child Behaviors and Experiences: A Meta-Analytic and Theoretical Review." *Psychological Bulletin* 128, no. 4 (2002): 539–79.

Gilliam, Walter S., Angela N. Maupin, Chin R. Reyes, Maria Accavitti, and Frederick Shic. *Do Early Educators' Implicit Biases Regarding Sex and Race Relate to Behavior Expectations and Recommendations of Preschool Expulsions and Suspensions?* Research Study Brief. New Haven, CT: Yale University Child Study Center, 2016.

Glaser, Clive. "Nostalgia for a Beating: Discipline, Generational Authority, and Corporal Punishment at a Soweto High School, c. 1960–2000." *History of Education* 48, no. 3 (2019): 395–409.

Glasser, William. *Control Theory: A New Explanation of How We Control Our Lives.* New York: Perennial Library, 1985.

Glasser, William. *Schools without Failure.* New York: Harper & Row, 1968.

Glenn, Myra C. "School Discipline and Punishment in Antebellum America." *Journal of the Early Republic* 1, no. 4 (1981): 395–408.

Glickman, Carl D., and Charles H. Wolfgang. *Solving Discipline Problems: Strategies for Classroom Teachers.* Boston: Allyn & Bacon, 1986.

Goff, Phillip A., Matthew C. Jackson, Brooke A. Di Leone, Carmen M. Culotta, and Natalie A. DiTomasso. "The Essence of Innocence: Consequences of Dehumanizing Black Children." *Journal of Personality and Social Psychology* 106, no. 4 (2014): 526–45.

Goodman, Joan F. "Is Punishment Passé?" *Education Week,* November 5, 2003.

Goodman, Joan F. "School Discipline in Moral Disarray." *Journal of Moral Education* 35, no. 2 (2006): 213–30.

Gordon, Nora. "Disproportionality in Student Discipline: Connecting Policy to Research." Brookings, January 22, 2018. https://www.brookings.edu/research/disproportionality-in-student-discipline-connecting-policy-to-research/.

Grant, Julia. *The Boy Problem: Educating Boys in Urban America, 1870–1970.* Baltimore: Johns Hopkins University Press, 2014.

Gregory, Anne, Russell J. Skiba, and Pedro A. Noguera. "The Achievement Gap and the Discipline Gap: Two Sides of the Same Coin?" *Educational Researcher* 39, no. 1 (January 2010): 59–68.

Greven, Philip. *The Protestant Temperament: Patterns of Child-Rearing, Religious Experience, and the Self in Early America.* Chicago: University of Chicago Press, 1977.

Grinspan, Jon. *The Virgin Vote: How Young Americans Made Democracy Social, Politics Personal, and Voting Popular in the Nineteenth Century.* Chapel Hill: University of North Carolina Press, 2016.

Grose, Francis, and Hewson Clarke, eds. *The 1811 Dictionary of the Vulgar Tongue*. Northfield, IL: Digest Books, 1971.

Haeckel, Ernst. *The Riddle of the Universe: At the Close of the Nineteenth Century*. New York: Harper, 1905.

Hall, G. Stanley. "Moral Training and Will-Training." *Pedagogical Seminary* 2, no. 1 (1892): 72–89.

Hall, Samuel Read. *Lectures on Schoolkeeping*. 3rd ed. Boston: Richardson, Lord & Holbrook, 1831.

Hall, Samuel Read. *Lectures on Schoolkeeping for Female Teachers*. Boston: Richardson, Lord & Holbrook, 1832.

Halttunen, Karen. "Humanitarianism and the Pornography of Pain in Anglo-American Culture." *American Historical Review* 100, no. 2 (April 1995): 303–34.

Hand, Michael. "Against Autonomy as an Educational Aim." *Oxford Review of Education* 32, no. 4 (2006): 535–50.

Hanna, Nathan. "Say What? A Critique of Expressive Retributivism." *Law and Philosophy: An International Journal for Jurisprudence and Legal Philosophy* 27, no. 2 (2008): 123–50.

Hart, H. L. A. "The Presidential Address: Prolegomenon to the Principles of Punishment." *Proceedings of the Aristotelian Society* 60 (1959): 1–26.

Hart, H. L. A. *Punishment and Responsibility: Essays in the Philosophy of Law*. New York: Oxford University Press, 1968.

Hartman, Andrew. *Education and the Cold War: The Battle for the American School*. New York: Palgrave Macmillan, 2008.

Hess, Frederick M., and Max C. Eden. "When School-Discipline 'Reform' Makes Schools Less Safe." *National Review*, December 15, 2017. https://www.nationalreview.com/2017/12/progressive-school-discipline-reform-hurting-students-parents/.

Hinton, Elizabeth. "'A War within Our Own Boundaries': Lyndon Johnson's Great Society and the Rise of the Carceral State." *Journal of American History* 102, no. 1 (June 2015): 100–112.

Hogan, David. "The Market Revolution and Disciplinary Power: Joseph Lancaster and the Psychology of the Early Classroom System." *History of Education Quarterly* 29, no. 3 (Autumn 1989): 381–417.

Hogan, David. "Modes of Discipline: Affective Individualism and Pedagogical Reform in New England, 1820–1850." *American Journal of Education* 99, no. 1 (November 1990): 1–56.

Hulbert, Ann. *Raising America: Experts, Parents, and a Century of Advice about Children*. New York: Alfred A. Knopf, 2003.

Human Rights Watch/ACLU. *Impairing Education: Corporal Punishment of Students with Disabilities in US Public Schools*. New York: Human Rights Watch, August 2009. https://www.aclu.org/files/pdfs/humanrights/impairingeducation.pdf.

Hume, David. *A Treatise of Human Nature*. Edited by L. A. Selby-Bigge. 2nd ed. Revised by P. H. Nidditch. Oxford: Clarendon Press, 1978.

Hutt, Ethan. *A Brief History of the Student Record*. New York: Ithaka S+R, September 6, 2016. http://www.sr.ithaka.org/wp-content/uploads/2016/09/SR_Report_Hutt_Brief_History_Student_Record_090616.pdf.

Hyman, Irwin, and Eileen MacDowell. "Introduction." In Hyman and Wise, *Corporal Punishment in American Education*, 3–22.

Hyman, Irwin A., and James H. Wise, eds. *Corporal Punishment in American Education*. Philadelphia: Temple University Press, 1979.

Igo, Sarah E. *The Known Citizen: A History of Privacy in Modern America*. Cambridge, MA: Harvard University Press, 2018.

Irving, Washington. *The Legend of Sleepy Hollow*. Indianapolis: Bobbs-Merill Company, 1906.

Itzkin, Elissa S. "Bentham's *Chrestomathia*: Utilitarian Legacy to English Education." *Journal of the History of Ideas* 39, no. 2 (April–June 1978): 303–31.

Jain, Sonia, Henrissa Bassey, Martha A. Brown, and Preety Kalra. *Restorative Justice in Oakland Schools: Implementation and Impacts*. Oakland, CA: Oakland Unified School District, 2014. https://www.ousd.org/cms/lib/CA01001176/Centricity/Domain/134/OUSD-RJ%20Report%20revised%20Final.pdf.

James, William. *Talks to Teachers on Psychology*. New York: Henry Holt, 1914.

Jewett, James P. "The Fight against Corporal Punishment in American Schools." *History of Education Journal* 4, no. 1 (Autumn 1952): 1–10.

Johnson, Clifton. *Old Time Schools and School-Books*. New York: MacMillan, 1904.

Jonas, Mark E., and Drew W. Chambers. "The Use and Abuses of Emulation as a Pedagogical Practice." *Educational Theory* 67, no. 3 (2017): 241–63.

Jones, Jacqueline. *Soldiers of Light and Love: Northern Teachers and Georgia Blacks, 1865–1873*. Athens: University of Georgia Press, 1980.

Jostyn, Jay. "The Manhasset Youth Council." *Journal of Educational Sociology* 18, no. 7 (March 1945): 417–25.

Kaestle, Carl F. *Pillars of the Republic: Common Schools and American Society*. New York: Hill & Wang, 1983.

Kaestle, Carl F. "Social Change, Discipline, and the Common School in Early Nineteenth-Century America." *Journal of Interdisciplinary History* 9, no. 1 (Summer 1978): 1–17.

Kafka, Judith. *The History of "Zero Tolerance" in American Public Schooling*. New York: Palgrave Macmillan, 2011.

Kant, Immanuel. "Justice and Punishment." Translated by W. Hastie. In Ezorsky, *Philosophical Perspectives on Punishment*, 102–6.

Katz, Michael B. *The Irony of Early School Reform: Educational Innovation in Mid-Nineteenth Century Massachusetts*. New York: Teachers College Press, 2001.

Kellogg, A. M. *School Management*. New York: E. L. Kellogg, 1884.

Kett, Joseph. *Merit: The History of a Founding Ideal from the American Revolution to the Twenty-First Century*. Ithaca, NY: Cornell University Press, 2013.

Kim, Catherine Y., Daniel J. Losen, and Damon T. Hewitt. *The School-to-Prison Pipeline: Structuring Legal Reform*. New York: New York University Press, 2010.

Koganzon, Rita. "'Contesting the Empire of Habit': Habituation and Liberty in Lockean Education." *American Political Science Review* 110, no. 3 (August 2016): 547–58.

Kohn, Alfie. *Beyond Discipline: From Compliance to Community*. Alexandria, VA: Association for Supervision and Curriculum Development, 1996.

Kohn, Alfie. *Unconditional Parenting: Moving from Rewards and Punishments to Love and Reason*. New York: Atria Books, 2006.

Kozol, Jonathan. *Death at an Early Age*. New York: New American Library, 1985.

Kupchik, Aaron. *The Real School Safety Problem*. Berkeley: University of California Press, 2016.

Kupchik, Aaron, and Nicole L. Bracy. "To Protect, Serve, and Mentor? Police Officers in Public Schools." In Monahan and Torres, *Schools under Surveillance*, 21–37.

Labaree, David F. *The Trouble with Ed Schools*. New Haven, CT: Yale University Press, 2004.

Lacoe, Johanna, and Matthew P. Steinberg. "Do Suspensions Affect Student Outcomes?" *Educational Evaluation and Policy Analysis* 41, no. 1 (2019): 34–62.

Lamboy, Lily, Ashley Taylor, and Winston Thompson. "Paternalistic Aims and (Mis)Attributions of Agency: What the Over-Punishment of Black Girls in U.S. Classrooms Teaches Us about Just School Discipline." *Theory and Research in Education* 18, no. 1 (2020): 59–77.

Lee, Harper. *To Kill a Mockingbird*. New York: J. B. Lippincott, 1960.

Lee, Virginia. "A Legal Analysis of *Ingraham v. Wright*." In Hyman and Wise, *Corporal Punishment in American Education*, 173–95.

Levinson, Meira. *The Demands of Liberal Education*. Oxford: Oxford University Press, 1999.

Levitan, Sar A., and Robert Taggart. "The Emergency Employment Act: An Interim Assessment." *Monthly Labor Review* 95, no. 6 (June 1972): 3–11.

Link, William A. *The Paradox of Southern Progressivism, 1880–1930*. Chapel Hill: University of North Carolina Press, 1992.

Lippmann, Walter. *Drift and Mastery: An Attempt to Diagnose the Current Unrest*. Englewood Cliffs, NJ: Prentice-Hall, 1961.

Locke, John. *Some Thoughts concerning Education and of the Conduct of the Understanding*. London: Hackett Classics, 1996.

Los Angeles Unified School District Records. University of California, Los Angeles Archives.

Losen, Daniel J., and Russell Skiba. *Suspended Education: Urban Middle Schools in Crisis*. Montgomery, AL: Southern Poverty Law Center, 2010.

Lustick, Hilary. "'Restorative Justice' or Restoring Order? Restorative School Discipline Practices in Urban Public Schools." *Urban Education* (November 2017): 1–28. https://doi.org/10.1177/0042085917741725.

Lyons, John F. *Teachers and Reform: Chicago Public Education, 1929–1970*. Urbana: University of Illinois Press, 2008.

MacIntyre, Alasdair. "How to Seem Virtuous without Actually Being So." In *Education in Morality*, edited by J. Mark Halstead and Terreance H. McLaughlin, 118–31. New York: Routledge, 2005.

MacLeod, David I. *The Age of the Child: Children in America, 1890–1920*. New York: Twayne, 1998.

Macready, Tom. "Learning Social Responsibility in Schools: A Restorative Practice." *Educational Psychology in Practice* 25, no. 3 (2009): 211–20.

Madison Teachers Incorporated. *Joint Committee on Safety and Discipline*. Madison, WI: Madison Metropolitan School District, 2015. http://www.madisonteachers.org/wp-content/uploads/2015/05/Joint-Committee-on-Safety-and-Discipline-Report-051315.pdf.

Manning, John. "Discipline in the Good Old Days." In Hyman and Wise, *Corporal Punishment in American Education*, 50–61.

Maslow, A. H. "A Theory of Human Motivation." *Psychological Review* 50, no. 4 (1943): 370–96.

Mather, Cotton. *Help for Distressed Parents*. Grand Rapids, MI: Soli Deo Gloria, 2004.

May, S. J. "Dedication of a Schoolhouse." *Common School Journal* 2, no. 14 (July 1840): 218–24.

McClay, Wilfred M. *The Masterless: Self & Society in Modern America*. Chapel Hill: University of North Carolina Press, 1994.

McClellan, B. Edward. *Moral Education in America: Schools and the Shaping of Character from Colonial Times to Present*. New York: Teachers College Press, 1999.

McCloskey, H. J. "A Non-Utilitarian Approach to Punishment." In Ezorsky, *Philosophical Perspectives on Punishment*, 119–34.

McCluskey, Gillean, Gwynedd Lloyd, Jean Kane, Sheila Riddell, Joan Stead, and Elisabet Weedon. "Can Restorative Practices in Schools Make a Difference?" *Educational Review* 60, no. 4 (2008): 405–17.

McGrew, Ken. "The Dangers of Pipeline Thinking: How the School-to-Prison Pipeline Metaphor Squeezes Out Complexity." *Educational Theory* 66, no. 3 (2016): 341–67.

McGrew, Ken. *Education's Prisoners: Schooling, the Political Economy, and the Prison Industrial Complex.* New York: Peter Lang, 2007.

McPherson, Thomas. "Punishment: Definition and Justification." *Analysis* 28, no. 1 (1967): 21–27.

Meek, Amy. "School Discipline 'As Part of the Teaching Process': Alternative and Compensatory Education Required by the State's Interest in Keeping Children in School." *Yale Law & Policy Review* 28, no. 1 (Fall 2009): 155–85.

Mehta, Jal. *The Allure of Order.* New York: Oxford University Press, 2013.

Mendible, Myra. *American Shame: Stigma and the Body Politic.* Bloomington: Indiana University Press, 2016.

Mill, John Stuart. *The Collected Works of John Stuart Mill.* Toronto: University of Toronto Press, 1991.

Mill, John Stuart. *On Liberty.* Boston: Ticknor & Fields, 1863.

Mintz, Steven. *Huck's Raft: A History of American Childhood.* Cambridge, MA: Belknap Press, 2004.

Mirel, Jeffrey. "The Traditional High School." *Education Next* 6, no. 1 (Winter 2006): 14–21.

Mitchell, Geana W., Leane B. Skinner, and Bonnie J. White. "Essential Soft Skills for Success in the Twenty-First Century Workforce as Perceived by Business Educators." *Delta Pi Epsilon Journal* 52, no. 1 (2010): 43–53.

Monahan, Torin, and Rodolfo Torres, eds. *Schools under Surveillance: Cultures of Control in Public Education.* New Brunswick, NJ: Rutgers University Press, 2010.

Morris, Edward W., and Brea L. Perry. "The Punishment Gap: School Suspension and Racial Disparities in Achievement." *Social Problems* 63, no. 1 (February 2016): 68–86.

Morris, Monique W. *Pushout: The Criminalization of Black Girls in Schools.* New York: New Press, 2016.

Morrison, Brenda E., and Dorothy Vaandering. "Restorative Justice: Pedagogy, Praxis, and Discipline." *Journal of School Violence* 11 (2012): 138–55.

Mukherjee, Elora. *Criminalizing the Classroom: The Over Policing of New York City Schools.* New York: New York Civil Liberties Union, 2007.

National Education Association Archives. George Washington University, Washington, DC.

National Research Council Committee on Deterrence and the Death Penalty. *Deterrence and the Death Penalty.* Edited by Daniel Nagin and John Pepper. Washington, DC: National Academies Press, 2012.

Neem, Johann. *Democracy's Schools: The Rise of Public Education in America.* Baltimore: Johns Hopkins University Press, 2017.

Neill, A. S. *Summerhill: A Radical Approach to Childrearing.* With a foreword by Erich Fromm. New York: Hart Publishing, 1960.

Neily, Clark. "One Test, Two Standards: The On-and-Off Role of 'Plausibility' in Rational Basis Review." *Georgetown Journal of Law & Public Policy* 4, no. 1 (2006): 199–212.

Newman, Anne. *Realizing Educational Rights: Advancing School Reform through Courts and Communities.* Chicago: University of Chicago Press, 2013.

Noddings, Nel. *Happiness and Education.* Cambridge: Cambridge University Press, 2005.

Noguera, Pedro A. "Schools, Prisons, and Social Implications of Punishment: Rethinking Disciplinary Practices." *Theory into Practice* 42, no. 4 (2003): 341–50.

Nolan, Kathleen. *Police in the Hallways: Discipline in an Urban American High School.* Minneapolis: University of Minnesota Press, 2011.

Noltemeyer, Amity L., and Rose Marie Ward. "Relationship between School Suspension and Student Outcomes: A Meta-Analysis." *School Psychology Review* 44, no. 2 (2015): 224–40.

Ohene, S. A., M. Ireland, C. McNeely, and I. W. Borowsky. "Parental Expectations, Physical Punishment, and Violence among Adolescents Who Score Positive on a Psychosocial Screening Test in Primary Care." *Pediatrics* 117, no. 2 (2006): 441–47.

Opal, J. M. "Academies and the Transformation of the Rural North, 1780s–1820s." *Journal of American History* 91, no. 2 (September 2004): 445–70.

Ozment, Steven E. *When Fathers Ruled: Family Life in Reformation Europe.* Cambridge, MA: Harvard University Press, 1983.

Parille, Ken. *Boys at Home: Discipline, Masculinity, and the "Boy-Problem" in Nineteenth-Century American Literature.* Knoxville: University of Tennessee Press, 2009.

Pearson, Susan J. *The Rights of the Defenseless: Protecting Animals and Children in Gilded Age America.* Chicago: University of Chicago Press, 2011.

Perrillo, Jonna. *Uncivil Rights: Teachers, Unions, and Race in the Battle for School Equity.* Chicago: University of Chicago Press, 2012.

Peshkin, Alan. *God's Choice: The Total World of a Fundamentalist Christian School.* Chicago: University of Chicago Press, 1986.

Peters, R. S. *Ethics and Education.* London: Allen & Unwin, 1966.

Petrilli, Michael. "A Supposed Discipline Fix Threatens School Cultures." *Education Next,* March 7, 2018. https://www.educationnext.org/supposed-discipline-fix-threatens-school-cultures-forum-petrilli/.

Petrina, Stephen. "The Medicalization of Education: A Historiographic Synthesis." *History of Education Quarterly* 46, no. 4 (Winter 2008): 503–31.

Pettinga, Gayle Lynn. "Rational Basis with Bite: Intermediate Scrutiny by Any Other Name." *Indiana Law Journal* 62, no. 3 (1987): 779–804.

Piele, Philip K. "Neither Corporal Punishment Cruel nor Due Process Due: The United States Supreme Court's Decision in *Ingraham v. Wright.*" In Hyman and Wise, *Corporal Punishment in American Education,* 91–106.

Pieper, Martha Heineman, and William Joseph Pieper. *Smart Love: The Compassionate Alternative to Discipline That Will Make You a Better Parent and Your Child a Better Person.* Boston, MA: Harvard Common Press, 1999.

Plotz, Judith. "The Perpetual Messiah: Romanticism, Childhood, and the Paradoxes of Human Development." In Finkelstein, *Regulated Children, Liberated Children,* 63–95.

Prince, John J. *School Management and Method, in Theory and Practice.* London: J. Heywood, 1886.

Provasnik, Stephen. "Judicial Activism and the Origins of Parental Choice: The Court's Role in the Institutionalization of Compulsory Education in the United States." *History of Education Quarterly* 46, no. 3 (Fall 2006): 311–47.

Raby, Rebecca. *School Rules: Obedience, Discipline, and Elusive Democracy.* Toronto: University of Toronto Press, 2012.

Ravitch, Diane. *Left Back: A Century of Failed School Reforms.* New York: Simon & Schuster, 2000.

Redfield, Sarah E., and Jason P. Nance. *School-to-Prison Pipeline: Preliminary Report, Part Two*. Chicago: American Bar Association, 2016.

Reese, William J. "The Origins of Progressive Education." *History of Education Quarterly* 41, no. 1 (Spring 2001): 1–24.

Reese, William J. *Testing Wars in the Public Schools: A Forgotten History*. Cambridge, MA: Harvard University Press, 2013.

Reich, Rob. *Bridging Liberalism and Multiculturalism in American Education*. Chicago: University of Chicago Press, 2002.

Renteln, Alison Dundes. "Corporal Punishment and the Cultural Defense." *Law and Contemporary Problems* 73, no. 2 (Spring 2010): 253–79.

Rentschler, Donald R. "Applying the Hand of Wisdom to the Seat of Learning: The 1974 Legislative Response in North Carolina." *High School Journal* 58, no. 8 (May 1975): 361–80.

Rhode, Joy. *Armed with Expertise: The Militarization of American Social Science Research during the Cold War*. Ithaca, NY: Cornell University Press, 2013.

Rios, Victor M. *Punished: Policing the Lives of Black and Latino Boys*. New York: New York University Press, 2011.

Roberts, Julian V., and Loretta J. Stalans. "Restorative Sentencing: Exploring the Views of the Public." *Social Justice Research* 17 (2004): 315–34.

Robles, Marcel M. "Executive Perceptions of the Top 10 Soft Skills Needed in Today's Workplace." *Business Communication Quarterly* 75, no. 4 (2012): 453–65.

Rousmaniere, Kate. *The Principal's Office: A Social History of the American School Principal*. Albany: State University of New York Press, 2013.

Rousmaniere, Kate, Kari Dehli, and Ning de Coninck-Smith, eds. *Discipline, Moral Regulation, and Schooling: A Social History*. New York: Garland Publishing, 1997.

Rush, Benjamin. *The Selected Writings of Benjamin Rush*. Edited by Dagobert D. Runes. New York: Philosophical Library, 1947.

Ryan, Francis T. "From Rod to Reason: Historical Perspectives on Corporal Punishment in Schools." *Educational Horizons* 72, no. 2 (Winter 1994): 70–77.

Schapiro, Robert A. "Polyphonic Federalism: State Constitutions in the Federal Courts." *California Law Review* 87, no. 6 (1999): 1411–68.

Schauer, Frederick. "Towards an Institutional First Amendment." *Minnesota Law Review* 89, no. 5 (2005): 1256–79.

Schlesinger, Elizabeth Bancroft. "Cotton Mather and His Children." *William and Mary Quarterly* 10, no. 2 (April 1953): 181–89.

Schneider, Jack. *From the Ivory Tower to the Schoolhouse: How Scholarship Becomes Common Knowledge in Education*. Cambridge, MA: Harvard Education Press, 2014.

Schumaker, Katie. *Troublemakers: Students' Rights and Racial Justice in the Long 1960s*. New York: New York University Press, 2019.

Scribner, Campbell F. *The Fight for Local Control: Schools, Suburbs, and American Democracy*. Ithaca, NY: Cornell University Press, 2016.

Sherman, Lawrence W., and Heather Strang. "Empathy for the Devil: The Nature and Nurture of Revenge." In *Emotions, Crime and Justice*, edited by Susanne Karstedt, Ian Loader, and Heather Strang, 145–68. Oxford: Hart Publishing, 2011.

Sherman, Lawrence W., and Heather Strang. *Restorative Justice: The Evidence*. London: Smith Institute, 2007. http://www.iirp.edu/pdf/RJ_full_report.pdf.

Shulman, Harry M. "Crime Prevention and the Public Schools." *Journal of Educational Sociology* 4 (October 1930): 69–81.

Simon, Sidney B., Leland Howe, and Howard Kirschenbaum. *Values Clarification: A Handbook of Practical Strategies for Teachers and Students.* New York: Hart, 1972.

Skiba, Russel, Lauren Shure, and Natasha Williams. *What Do We Know about Racial and Ethnic Disproportionality in School Suspension and Expulsion?* New York: Atlantic Philanthropies, 2011.

Skiba, Russell J., Mariella I. Arredondo, Chrystal Gray, and M. Karega Rausch. "What Do We Know about Discipline Disparities? New and Emerging Research." In *Inequality in School Discipline: Research and Practice to Reduce Disparities,* edited by Russell Skiba, Kavitha Mediratta, and M. Karega Rausch, 21–38. New York: Palgrave Macmillan, 2016.

Skinner, B. F. *Beyond Freedom and Dignity.* New York: Bantam/Vintage, 1972.

Skinner, B. F. *Walden Two.* New York: MacMillan, 1948.

Southey, Robert. "Fox, *A Comparative View of the Plans of Education as Detailed in the Publications of Dr. Bell and Mr. Lancaster, and Remarks on Dr. Bell's Madras School, and Hints to the Managers and Committees of Charity and Sunday Schools, on the Practicability of Extending Such Institutions upon Mr. Lancaster's Plan.*" *Quarterly Review* 6, no. 11 (1811): 264–304.

Southey, Robert. *The Origin, Nature, and Object, of the New System of Education.* London: John Murray, 1812.

Speicher, Allison. "The School of One Scholar: Schoolmistress-Schoolboy Romance in the Nineteenth-Century School Story." *Children's Literature Association Quarterly* 42, no. 1 (Spring 2017): 3–20.

Sprigge, T. L. S. "A Utilitarian Reply to Dr. McCloskey." In Ezorsky, *Philosophical Perspectives on Punishment,* 66–79.

Stearns, Peter N., and Clio Stearns. "American Schools and the Uses of Shame: An Ambiguous History." *History of Education* 46, no. 1 (April 2016): 58–75.

Steffes, Tracy. *School, Society, and State: A New Education to Govern Modern America, 1890–1940.* Chicago: University of Chicago Press, 2012.

Stein, Abe B. "Adolescent Participation in Community Co-ordinating Councils." *Journal of Educational Sociology* 21, no. 3 (November 1947): 177–83.

Stevenson, Louise. *The Victorian Homefront: American Thought and Culture, 1860–1880.* Ithaca, NY: Cornell University Press, 2001.

Straus, Murray. *Beating the Devil out of Them: Corporal Punishment in American Families.* Lanham, MD: Lexington Books, 1994.

Strober, Myra, and David Tyack. "Why Do Women Teach and Men Manage?" *Signs* 5, no. 3 (Spring 1980): 494–503.

Stuntz, William J. *The Collapse of American Criminal Justice.* Cambridge, MA: Belknap Press of Harvard University Press, 2011.

Superfine, Benjamin Michael. "The Evolving Role of the Courts in Educational Policy: The Tension between Judicial, Scientific, and Democratic Decision Making in *Kitzmiller v. Dover.*" *American Educational Research Journal* 46, no. 4 (December 2009): 898–923.

Sutton, John R. *Stubborn Children: Controlling Delinquency in the United States, 1640–1981.* Berkeley: University of California Press, 1988.

Tafa, Elmon M. "Corporal Punishment: The Brutal Face of Botswana's Authoritarian Schools." *Educational Review* 54, no. 1 (2002): 17–26.

Tanenhaus, David S. *The Constitutional Rights of Children:* In re Gault *and Juvenile Justice.* Lawrence: University Press of Kansas, 2011.

Tavuchis, Nicholas. *Mea Culpa: A Sociology of Apology and Reconciliation.* Stanford, CA: Stanford University Press, 1991.

Taylor, J. S. *Art of Class Management and Discipline.* New York: E. L. Kellogg, 1903.

Theobald, Paul. *Call School: Rural Education in the Midwest to 1918.* Carbondale: Southern Illinois University Press, 1995.

Theobald, Paul. "Country School Curriculum and Governance: The One-Room School Experience in the Nineteenth-Century Midwest." *American Journal of Education* 101, no. 2 (February 1993): 116–39.

Tocqueville, Alexis de. *Democracy in America.* Translated by Harvey C. Mansfield and Delba Winthrop. Chicago: University of Chicago Press, 2000.

Tropea, Joseph. "Bureaucratic Order and Special Children: Urban Schools, 1890s–1940s." *History of Education Quarterly* 27, no. 1 (Spring 1987): 29–53.

Tyack, David. *The One Best System: A History of American Urban Education.* Cambridge, MA: Harvard University Press, 1974.

Tyack, David, and Elizabeth Hansot. *Learning Together: A History of Coeducation in American Schools.* New Haven, CT: Yale University Press, 1990.

United States Government Accountability Office. *Discipline Disparities for Black Students, Boys, and Students with Disabilities.* Washington, DC: United States Government Accountability Office, March 2018. https://www.gao.gov/assets/700/690828.pdf.

Upton, Dell. "Lancasterian Schools, Republican Citizenship, and the Spatial Imagination in Early Nineteenth-Century America." *Journal of the Society of Architectural Historians* 55, no. 3 (September 1996): 238–53.

Vogler, Pen. "The Poor Child's Friend." *History Today* 65, no. 2 (February 2015): 4–5. https://www.historytoday.com/pen-vogler/poor-child%E2%80%99s-friend.

von Hirsch, Andrew. *Censure and Sanctions.* Oxford: Clarendon Press, 1993.

Warnick, Bryan R. *Understanding Student Rights in Schools: Speech, Religion, and Privacy in Educational Settings.* New York: Teachers College Press, 2013.

Weaver, Richard. "Education and the Individual." *Intercollegiate Review* 2, no. 1 (September 1965): 68–76.

Weiss, Carolyn Peri. "Curbing Violence or Teaching It: Criminal Immunity for Teachers Who Inflict Corporal Punishment." *Washington University Law Review* 74, no. 4 (January 1996): 1251–89.

West, Elliott. *Growing Up with the Country: Childhood on the Far Western Frontier.* Albuquerque: University of New Mexico Press, 1989.

Westbrook, Robert B. *John Dewey and American Democracy.* Ithaca, NY: Cornell University Press, 1991.

Wexler, Jay D. "Defending the Middle Way: Intermediate Scrutiny as Judicial Minimalism." *George Washington Law Review* 66 (1998): 298–352.

White, Emerson Elbridge. *School Management.* New York: American Book Company, 1893.

Whitman, Walt. "Death in the Schoolroom: A Fact." *Democratic Review* no. 9 (August 1841): 177–81.

Winslow, Hubbard. "On the Dangerous Tendency to Innovations and Extremes in Education." In *Introductory Discourse and the Lectures Delivered before the American Institute of Instruction,* 169–88. Boston: Carter, Hendee & Co., 1835.

Woolfolk, Robert L. *The Value of Psychotherapy: The Talking Cure in an Age of Clinical Science*. New York: Guilford Press, 2005.

Wright, Arthur D., and George E. Gardner. *Hall's Lectures on School-Keeping*. Hanover, NH: Dartmouth University Press, 1929.

Wringe, Bill. *An Expressive Theory of Punishment*. Houndmills, Basingstoke, Hampshire: Palgrave Macmillan, 2016.

Zehr, Howard. *Changing Lenses: A New Focus for Crime and Justice*. Scottdale, PA: Herald Press, 1990.

Zilversmit, Arthur. *Changing Schools: Progressive Education Theory and Practice, 1930–1960*. Chicago: University of Chicago Press, 1993.

Zimmerman, Jonathan. *Small Wonder: The Little Red Schoolhouse in History and Memory*. New Haven, CT: Yale University Press, 2009.

Index

Made in United States
Orlando, FL
13 May 2024

46832890R00100